THE SYRIAN UPRISING

St Andrews Papers
on Contemporary Syria

SERIES EDITOR, RAYMOND HINNEBUSCH

THE SYRIAN UPRISING

Dynamics of an Insurgency

Carsten Wieland
Adam Almqvist
Helena Nassif

University of St Andrews Centre for Syrian Studies

© 2013 by the University of St Andrews Centre for Syrian Studies

Published by the University of St Andrews Centre for Syrian Studies
School of International Relations
Fife, Scotland
UK

All rights reserved. No part of this publication may be reproduced or
transmitted in any form or by any means without prior permission of the publisher.

Distributed throughout the world by
Lynne Rienner Publishers, Inc.
1800 30th Street
Boulder, CO 80301
USA
www.rienner.com

British Library Cataloguing-in-Publication Data
A catalogue record for this book is available from the British Library.

Printed and bound in the United States of America

ISBN: 978-0-9568732-1-7

Contents

	Foreword *Tina Zintl*	1
1	Asad's Decade of Lost Chances *Carsten Wieland*	5
2	The Syrian Uprising and the Transnational Public Sphere: Transforming the Conflict in Syria *Adam Almqvist*	47
3	Celebrity Politics in Troubled Times: The Case of Muna Wassef *Helena Nassif*	79
	Appendix: Memorandum of the Advisory Committee about the Internal Situation on the Verge of the Second Decade of the Leadership of Your Excellency	95

References 109
About the Authors 115

Foreword
Tina Zintl

In this issue of the St Andrews Papers, three excellent articles – each based on empirical information collected in interviews with Syrian respondents – as well as an internal whitepaper by a presidential advisory committee share remarkable insights on the first months of the Syrian uprising that begun in March 2011. Though the articles take very different perspectives, i.e. on the transnational public space, on an individual artist's divided loyalties as well as a retrospective state-centred point of view, they all show the inconsistencies and contradictions the Syrian political system was afflicted with and which, ultimately, were brought to the fore and aggravated by the uprising.

Carsten Wieland demonstrates at which points of his rule and how Bashar al-Asad could have taken a different route down history. Wieland's counterfactual analysis thus emphasizes that there were several lost opportunities which became particularly obvious in retrospect. For instance, what seemed, at first, like a comeback to the international stage, carefully orchestrated by the Syrian regime from the 2008 onwards, was 'wasted' and not translated into corresponding domestic political reform. With the advent of the uprising even these earlier gains were one-by-one readily given up to a confrontative foreign policy. Viewed in this way, the Syrian regime's inept manoeuvring during the first months of the uprising was a continuation of its earlier politics of 'lost chances'.

Adam Almqvist's and Helena Nassif's contributions both demonstrate how the Syrian public space developed during the early uprising and, by doing so, illuminate the dilemmas and limited room for action two particular groups of people faced, cyberactivists and internationally-known celebrities. This is particularly interesting since both the diaspora and artists are at times perceived as actors who are 'independent' enough – geographically and intellectually – to formulate political demands and, thus, to possibly constitute a democratizing force.

As Almqvist shows, expatriate cyberactivists have been playing a significant role since the beginning of the uprising and they have had a clear influence on both the nature of the transnational public sphere and on the situation on the ground. Partly mobilizing the protests against al-Asad's rule, partly documenting them and spreading them to foreign media outlets, they forced the Syrian regime to fight back on the transnational public front as well. On the one hand, cyberactivists are just one group of several groups of transnational Syrians spurred into action by the uprising and confronted with questions of representativeness and internal factionalism. On the other hand, even though they were unable to turn the tables in favour of the oppositional struggle, the uprising has developed a distinct transnational twist through them.

Helena Nassif focuses on the Syrian actress Muna Wassef and her publicly made statements and actions during the early days of the uprising. Being the mother of exiled activist Ammar Abdulhamid, the famous actress sought to use her popularity to rally humanitarian aid for the suffering civilian population in Daraa; additionally, her famous role as an anti-imperialist heroine in a TV series made protesters project their hopes onto her. Yet, as the contribution vividly shows, the al-Asad regime continued to have a powerful hand in the entertainment industry, and knew how to discredit such calls. The contribution thereby allows the drawing of conclusions on Syrian society beyond Mouna Wassef's particular biography. Central bones of contention in the current crisis, e.g. the cleavage between 'inside' and 'outside' as well as the fear of sectarian strife, can be viewed through her. The first is reflected by Wassef's rootedness in Syria vs. her affection for her oppositionist son living abroad; the second was demonstrated by protesters' creative use of her fictional role as a strong Christian woman, thus trying to resist the increasingly sectarian nature of the protests.

Lastly, the memorandum in the annex, prepared in 2010, had been commissioned by the Syrian president's office but was later ignored by it. While the short-timed and ineffectual nature of advisory committees and their reports was rather common under Bashar al-Asad – their recommendations were regularly sought but seldom implemented – the frankness and urgency demonstrated by this particular report are striking. It shows that 'insiders' of the system were well aware of the headwinds al-Asad's politics and, particularly, his polarizing political economy faced. Despite due adulation of its recipient, the memorandum to the president spells out that "difficulties [...] have escalated, by neglect and mismanagement, into a socio-economic crisis" and thus led to "a great deal of dissatisfaction among the citizens as well as the elite."

For instance, the memorandum points towards the lack of direction and clear decision-making, rising poverty and social imbalance, corruption and mismanagement and, even, towards the limits of using police, security services and the military for controlling social unrest. It prefigures the outbreak of the popular uprising less than a year later and, notably, it is a far cry from the self-assured public speeches of Bashar al-Asad. As late as end-January 2011 he claimed in a, by now infamous, interview with the Wall Street Journal that "[i]f you want to talk about Tunisia and Egypt, we are outside of this" since he believed himself to be "very closely linked to the beliefs of the [Syrian] people".[1] Thus, the memorandum presents a highly interesting primary source that not only confirms Carsten Wieland's point that Bashar al-Asad *could* have taken different decisions and possibly even have warded off the uprising, but that also demonstrates that the Syrian president *was informed* by his advisors about the most pressing problems and the alternatives available to him.

The different perspectives presented in "The Syrian Uprising: Dynamics of an Insurgency" illustrate which structural problems and misguided tactics led up to the current crisis and they help to explain the downward spiral of brutality that followed in the subsequent months, turning the spontaneous popular uprising into a protracted conflict.

---

[1] The Wall Street Journal, 31.01.2011: "Interview with Syrian President Bashar al-Assad", available from http://online.wsj.com/article/%20SB10001424052748703833204576114712441122894.html, last accessed 07.05.2011.

1
Asad's Decade of Lost Chances[1]
Carsten Wieland

The autocrats who were toppled during the Arab Spring had persevered for some 30 or 40 years before their power structure imploded. After only a decade of rule, the Syrian regime under President Bashar al-Asad seems to be nearing its end. The country, its morale and social fabric, are in ruins. Born in 1965 Asad is the youngest among the Arab autocrats and already politically paralyzed - no matter with which scenario the bloody revolt in his country will end. How has this happened after Asad started his rule with so much anticipation and high hopes in June 2000? The story of his political career is a chain of missed chances and practical failures.

We can assess how far Asad has fallen when we compare it to where he came from after the death of his father, Hafez. For this purpose I would like to quote a passage from my book "Ballots or Bullets?" in which I reflected the mood in the streets of Damascus some eight years ago:

> Although his nimbus is fading, the young president possesses an image that, from the point of view of most Syrians, is neither stained with blood nor corrupted by radicalism or incompetence (though some would say more the latter than the former). He has successfully been able to distance himself from his father's political Stone Age. Most Syrians tend to look for faults in Bashar's surroundings rather than in Bashar himself.[2]

After 2011 the president will never be able to revive his former image. He has chosen bullets instead of ballots.

Usually, any assessment of Bashar al-Asad starts with his personality, although this approach fails to explain developments in their complexity. "Bashar is not the regime", traditional oppositional figures used to reiterate. This was different under Hafez al-Asad. Bashar's regime is a complex web of direct or subtle influences, priorities, jealousies and power struggles. There are indications that at times Bashar was incapable of enacting decisions of his own or even fulfilling given promises, because others were calling the shots. A leading and well-informed oppositional figure said at the end of 2010 that Asad had been left to act freely in foreign policy only, whereas domestically the secret services, the Baath Party, his clan and big business representatives were controlling the sinecure.[3]

Without further evidence it is hard to prove if the observations also held true a few months later. In light of this thesis it remains an open question as to what extent the cruelty of 2011 and 2012 and the numerous technical mistakes committed in suppressing the popular protests are due to the plurality of power centres in the Syrian polity under Asad or if they can be directly attributed to him and his personal strategy. Whether he is personally responsible for each and every shot that was fired, for each child that was tortured and mutilated, for every armed attack of the *shabbiha* Alawite gangs to incite sectarian hatred, for cattle and fields that were burnt to starve dissenting villagers, does not really matter in the end. Since 2000 the president has reshuffled almost all important positions in the *mukhabarat*, the military and government bureaucracy. He is the president and thus responsible for the so-called security solution. The protests triggered typical reflexes of a thoroughly authoritarian culture with a cruel history of civil wars and crackdowns. Survival is a zero-sum game where the winner takes it all.

This outcome was far from inevitable as the following pages show. Asad had a plethora of opportunities that he missed one by one, domestically and internationally. Many Syrians pinned their hopes on the young president as a reformer (as their fathers and grandfathers had already projected their hopes on Hafez al-Asad as a "liberalizer" and "pragmatist" in 1970-1971). From the beginning of his rule in 2000 Bashar faced a very moderate and intellectual opposition that did not pursue the priority of toppling the president but that tried to press for incremental change and gradual pluralism. Bashar did not reach out to them but launched three major waves of suppression against the oppositional Civil Society Movement between 2001 and 2008-2009. The noose was tightening around the neck of the opposition despite increasing relaxation of international relations from 2008 onwards. Syria was by no means on a path of reform when the Arab Spring hit the country. Nevertheless, the international community was ready to listen to Bashar's promises and to appreciate the certain stability that he embodied until he was rolled over by mass protests from March 2011 onwards. Bashar led his country into international isolation and traumatic destruction. Stability and secularism, the Asads' main assets, are no more. Asad destroyed his political legacy, his family, his religious community, Syria as it used to be and probably himself. The decade of his rule is a tragic story because it could have ended so differently.

The Loss of Projected Innocence

The trained ophthalmologist - often described as western in outlook because of his studies in the United Kingdom - differs from the stereotype of a brutal dictator. In his youth he is reported to have been relatively humble, honest, and even "non-ideological".[4] He did not display anything similar to the arrogant, dissolute, and excessive lifestyles of the sons of the former Iraqi President Saddam Hussein or Libya's Revolutionary Leader Muammar al-Qaddafi. Asad is no natural leader and did not intend to get involved in politics. He had to follow his father's will after the premature death of his elder brother Basil in a car accident in 1994. Asad was more interested in the internet and computers than in conspiracies and arms. In one of the most sealed off countries ruled by the "Sphinx of Damascus"[5], his father Hafez al-Asad, he became head of the Syrian Computer Society from which he later recruited some of his governing personnel.

Contrasted with the unscrupulous "security solution" against the mostly peaceful street protests of his own people in 2011, the following statements of Asad in his inauguration speech a decade earlier appear almost surreal:

> I am not after any post nor do I avoid any responsibility. The post is not an end but a means to achieve an end. And now, and since my people have honored me with their choice of me as president of the Republic [...] I would like to say that I have assumed the post but I have not occupied the position [...]. I feel that the man you have known [...] will not change at all once he assumes his post. He came out of the people and lived with them and shall remain one of them. You may expect to see him everywhere whether in the work place or in the streets or at your picnics in order to learn from you [...]. The man who has become a president is the same man who was a doctor and an officer and first and foremost is a citizen.[6]

Indeed, Asad was seen at times in the lanes of old Damascus or Aleppo without visible bodyguards and dining in restaurants.

If assertions of Sheikh Ahmed Badr al-Din Hassoun, the Syrian Grand Mufti, reflect the truth, Asad confided in him more than once that in his dreams he would like to return to his profession one day and run an eye clinic. This was the first time that a confidant of the president had spoken of the possibility of a voluntary and premature end to his rule (although the remarkable utterances may have had tactical reasons in the tense political situation of November 2011).[7]

Indeed, Asad had not been known for his brutality and extravagance but for precisely the opposite: his restraint in private matters, awkwardness in public appearances, and even political ineptness up to the point that during the gravest crisis of his political life the media described him as "the dictator who cannot dictate."[8] A member of the opposition reported already years ago that some had complained about his "weak character." "He holds the opinion of the person he last spoke to," said an oppositional journalist who preferred to remain anonymous. His sister Bushra reportedly called him "stupid and nervous" when he allegedly was among a circle of relatives after the turbulent events in Lebanon in early 2005.[9]

Certainly, Asad has made a plethora of technical and strategic mistakes. After a decade of his rule everything pointed to the fact that despite his differences, he ended up sharing the other Arab autocrats' cynicism, loss of reality and – contrary to his and Hassoun's statements – an autocrat with an apocalyptic outlook and will to cling to power at any cost.

The cynicism is reflected in his readiness to accept an unexpectedly high blood toll and to give carte blanche to the security forces and Alawi militias. A researcher close to the Syrian opposition said that during the uprising Asad calmly explained that his strategy was to allow not more than 25 to 30 people killed per day, on Fridays maybe more, in order to avoid upsetting international public opinion.[10] With several thousands of people killed since March 2011 as well as tens of thousands arrested and held under torture and abysmal conditions in cramped dungeons or sport stadiums (estimates from fall 2011 range from 20,000 to 50,000), it is possible that the number will equal the toll of the notorious massacre in Hama in 1982. The cruelty of tortures, rapes, collective punishment, the barring of wounded from treatment, and the cold-bloodedness of civilian killings in the streets of Syrian towns that are documented in countless amateur videos, despite the technical obstacles and personal risks, exceeds what the world had witnessed in the Libyan civil war that led to the fall of Qaddafi. Even worse, the displayed degree of atrocities against a widely unarmed population is not at all necessary to suppress a rebellion. Technically speaking, it is counterproductive. But we will come back to bad management and political mistakes during the upheaval later in the article.

Asad's increasing loss of reality is well demonstrated in an interview that he gave to the *Wall Street Journal* on January 31. The president said that Arab rulers would need to move faster to accommodate the rising political and economic aspirations of Arab peoples: "If you did not see the need for reform before what happened in Egypt and in Tunisia, it is too late to do any reform," he chided his fellow leaders. Then Asad assured the interviewer (and perhaps himself):

> We have more difficult circumstances than most of the Arab countries but in spite of that Syria is stable. Why? Because you have to be very closely linked to the beliefs of the people. This is the core issue. When there is divergence between your policy and the people's beliefs and interests, you will have this vacuum that creates disturbances. So people do not only live on interests; they also live on beliefs, especially in very ideological areas. Unless you understand the ideological aspect of the region, you cannot understand what is happening.

In the lengthy interview the president also reflected on his people who were not yet ready for reform:

> We still have a long way to go because it is a process. If I was brought up in different circumstances, I [would] have to train myself and, to be realistic, we have to wait for the next generation to bring this reform. [...] If you want to be transparent with your people, do not do anything cosmetic, whether to deceive your people or to get some applau[se] from the West. They want to criticize you, let them criticize and do not worry. [...] I do not think it is about time [for faster political reform, representation of people, and improving human rights], it is about the hope, because if I say that in five years' time or ten years' time may be, if the situation is going to be better, people are patient in our region.[11]

Not even two months later, the people's patience ran out and confrontations between protesters and security forces across Syria shook the Baathist regime more than any challenge since the 1980s. And his first public appearance was as a smiling president, surrounded by parliamentarian *claqueurs*, who made a surreal speech in the Syrian parliament at the end of March. Meanwhile, the Syria known for decades had already ceased to exist. The protests have torn asunder the delicate fabric of rules, explicit and implicit, that for decades had determined the relations between the regime and the citizenry. In the end, the nationalistic discourse, the antagonism with Israel and the West in general, and the pro-Palestinian rhetoric did not outweigh the daily social and economic grievances, the wish for the end of tutelage, and all this combined with the loss of fear after the successful popular uprisings in Tunisia and Egypt. The internal enemy overshadowed the external one to the surprise of many observers inside and outside Syria.

Ironically, it was Asad himself who made this form of upheaval possible in the first place. He became victim of his own modernization. By allowing satellite dishes, the internet, and by fostering a modern communication infrastructure, albeit all in the hands of his clan, he created a modern form of protest movement that exchanges videos via *YouTube* and organizes itself via *Facebook* and SMS. Though several internet sites are permanently blocked, Syrians have far more access to information and the outside world, through satellite TV, blogs and foreign media. Precisely these visible signs of modernization caused hope among many young Syrians for further changes and at the same time nurtured the yearning for more freedoms when Asad took power.

The country had indeed made some progress during the ten years of Asad's rule in areas that do not touch upon matters like democracy or human rights. Syrian media outlets were more numerous and plainspoken than under Hafez, provided that they did not cross red lines related to politics, religion and sex. Arts and letters benefited from more freedom of expression. Cell phones and other modern equipment became accessible to a wider range of people. Women's organizations gained strength and were granted room to maneuver even if they were not legally registered or explicitly supportive of the government.

Clearly, the development of the country under Asad had been an asymmetric one. Whereas reforms became visible especially in the macro-economic realm, a stand-still or even reversal could be observed in the political, administrative, and socio-economic arenas. After political pluralisation seemed too risky the president reduced his aspirations first to administrative reforms (anti-corruption, efficiency, etc.), and when this was met with resistance, he concentrated on economic reforms that had been moving along a bumpy road since they began but were indispensable for the regime's survival.

Internationally speaking, Syria's development in the past decade had taken place in unusually harsh and not entirely predictable conditions. The 9/11 attacks in Washington and New York in 2001 changed the whole board game in the Middle East and beyond, aggravated by the military approach of the US administration under President George W. Bush. No democratic experiment was going to be tolerated in Syria as US threats of regime change began to emerge in 2002, and the Baathist regime entrenched itself in ideological opposition to the Iraq war. Pressure mounted on Syria from abroad, especially from Saudi Arabia, France and the United States in subsequent years, culminating in the UN Security Council Resolution 1559, calling upon "all remaining foreign forces to withdraw from Lebanon." Asad began to lose his nerve and pursued an abrasive policy towards Lebanon. This culminated in the assassination of Lebanese Prime Minister Rafiq Hariri in February 2005, which aggravated Syria's isolation and entailed the forced withdrawal of Syrian troops from Lebanon.

Asad used to cite these events to justify the delay of domestic reforms. "We were affected by the situation in Iraq or in Lebanon. There are many things that we wanted to do in 2005 we are planning to do in the year 2012, seven years later! It is not realistic to have a time frame because you are not living in a situation where you can control the events", he said in the *WSJ* interview at the end of January 2011.[12] He is definitely right about the fact that the foreign policy environment and the approach of some western countries in the region were not at all conducive to the opening up of minds and policies in Syria. But despite a series of external shocks, many mistakes were homemade.

Sticking to the Baath Path and a Narrowing Circle of Trust

The chain of possible chances starts right at the beginning of Asad's rule. The first opportunity to change course occurred when the young heir to the republican throne was still highly dependent on the apparatus of his father. He could not be sure how supportive the power circles would be if he deviated too quickly from the trodden path of Baathism. Asad was dependent on key players of the old power structure who changed Syria's constitution to the effect that Asad could become president at 34 years instead of the previously necessary 40 years of age. Theoretically, however, Asad could have tried to put his legitimacy on a wider basis by instituting himself as a transitional president who would call for a popular vote. Since there was no other candidate around and much less any organized party, he would have won by a landslide.

But any direct election would have called into question the Baath system as a whole that had served his father as a stable basis for three decades and enabled the smooth succession. Moreover, competition from within the family ranks was still looming. His uncle, Rifat al-Asad (who was exiled in 1984 after openly contesting Hafez al-Asad's rule), for example, never really thought that Bashar was the right man for the job. He could have taken advantage of any mistake or volatility to snatch power himself. Similar ambitions could have emerged in the security apparatus or with other major political protagonists like long-time Vice

President Abdulhalim Khaddam (who defected in 2005), or Syria's experienced Foreign Minister Farouq al-Shara.

Asad chose to stick to the Baath path. In reality, however, the Baath discourse camouflaged the ideological erosion of the system. There was not much left of socialism and neither of pan-Arabism. Asad weakened the influence of the Baath Party further during his rule but he never questioned the foundations of the system as such. Still, power relations had been renegotiated, and Baathist functionaries have been sidelined. In times of crisis the circle of persons that the Asad clan can trust has been contracting more and more up to the point that if the erosion escalates, it may become difficult to recruit enough staunch and qualified loyalists to effectively run the country.

In the years leading to the crisis, the circle of trust had been narrowing. The regime developed increasingly primordial features; it has become more Alawi compared to Hafez's times.[13] Interestingly, the second layer of regime functionaries after the Alawi avant-garde is composed of personalities from the Houran (especially Dera'a), including the Vice President and longtime foreign minister, Farouq al-Shara, who is a Sunni. Given the cruel events in Dera'a, this second layer of functionaries in the regime apparatus may prove less reliable in the future. Shara is still a man of the regime without any doubt, but he is rumoured to have had a difference of opinion with Bashar and especially Maher al-Asad on the crackdown in Dera'a. The communiqué of the foreign Syrian opposition after their conference in the Turkish city of Antalya in June called for handing over power to the vice president.

Louay Hussein, secular editor and leading figure of Syria's domestic opposition, shed light on the differences of Bashar and Hafez al-Asad's regimes in a conversation in October 2010. According to Hussein, the father was able to build his legitimacy on two pillars: social development and the liberation of occupied territories (or at least the attempt to do so). He had the power to control the Islamists and was ready to fight. "Bashar was handed power on a silver plate", Hussein said. He has been lacking the two pillars of his father. The younger group had "no knowledge and vision of the state's identity. They are playing around. They don't know what losing means because they didn't fight for anything and didn't face any real challenges."[14] The moment to fight came unexpectedly, and it turned out that the system was exclusively based on hard power, i.e. on the extinction of dissenters and threats.[15]

Crushing the Damascus Spring: The Failure of National Reconciliation

A second opportunity to pursue sweeping changes was to come soon after Asad's assumption of power. In his inaugural speech he called for Syrians to actively contribute to shaping the country's future.[16] Intellectuals were inspired and began to discuss more and more freely in the newly-found debating clubs in the halls of private houses. The dynamics that emerged thereof in September 2000 became known as the Damascus Spring. That fall, the Christian writer Michel Kilo headed a group of intellectuals who published the "manifesto of the 99," followed in December by the "manifesto of the 1,000." The secular philosopher, Sadiq al-Azm, was one of the key signatories. Riad Seif, an entrepreneur and outspoken Member of Parliament, went the furthest, putting forward social-democratic ideals of a "fair market economy" that he upheld with decent labor practices in the companies he owned. Politically, he called for a constitutional state, an independent legislature and courts, and a free press. But Seif crossed a red line when he announced his intention to found a party of his own. He was arrested, and the Damascus Spring turned cold as the debating clubs in Damascus had to close down one after the other.

Had the Syrians listened more carefully to Asad's inaugural speech, they may have anticipated that it was modernization that was on the new president's agenda but not sweeping political reforms, much less democracy. In this speech in June 2000, Asad had made his position clear.

> We cannot apply the democracy of others to ourselves. Western democracy, for example, is the outcome of a long history that resulted in customs and traditions, which distinguish the current culture of Western societies. […] We have to have our democratic experience which is special to us, which stems from our history, culture, civilization, and which is a response to the needs of our society and the requirements of our reality.[17]

Simply, this meant that the Baath Party was to retain political leadership. In reply to questions about political reform, the president later answered with stilted formulations such as: "We need an intellectual basis. There should be a connection between the political proposal and the social structure in society."[18] And the latter, he implied, was not yet mature enough to enable the population to participate in politics as in a Western-style democracy. These are the very same thoughts that he reiterated in the interview with the WSJ in January 2011.

At the very beginning of his rule Asad plugged into the notorious discourse of other Arab autocrats in the region: Their people were not ready for democracy, and democracy was a "cultural phenomenon" of the west. In the Arab Spring of 2011 the people finally showed that, indeed, they were ready not only for practical changes but also for a new political discourse and even political culture. People demonstrated that it was their rulers who were responsible for keeping them in a state of poverty and deliberate political immaturity.

Although the mostly elderly protagonists of the Civil Society Movement exchanged ideological views sometimes cut off from the discourse of younger people, the far-sightedness and intellectual maturity of the Syrian opposition's discourse became clear unexpectedly ten years after the suffocation of the Damascus Spring. Sadiq al-Azm draws a parallel between the Arab Spring of 2011 and the Damascus Spring of 2001:

> The Charter of 99 contained all the slogans, demands and aspirations wherever there is an intifada now. The Damascus Spring created the first documents that emphasized freedom, democracy, human rights, civil society and so on, and avoided the typical attacks on Israel. The Damascus Spring was a dress rehearsal of the Arab Spring.

The philosopher, who lives in Beirut now, observes a maturation of Arab society during the upheavals: "It was the regimes that represented themselves as representatives of enlightenment and state rationalism, and suddenly they clung to conspiracy theories and kept repeating them mindlessly, not the simple masses who had always been blamed for falling prey to conspiracies."[19]

Despite his young age Bashar al-Asad did not distinguish himself from his elder counterparts. He rather tried to follow the Chinese example: economic liberalization without, or with only minor, political reforms at home — or bread before freedom, as expressed by Riad Seif.[20] It took many Syrians and observers of Syria a long time to realize that, in the end, Asad was aiming at bread *instead of* freedom.

The clampdown of the Damascus Spring in 2001 was the first wave of suppression against the moderate Syrian opposition. Asad decided to prioritize regime stability before democratic experiments. This was a conscious step to secure his power after he felt he would lose control. The then Vice-president Abdulhalim Khaddam was instrumental in putting the brakes on the development, and the Civil Society Movement went underground - in the Syrian context more appropriately put: into the tea houses. Café Rawda was the most popular meeting point right around the corner of the parliament building. For the next couple of years the regime and the leftist intellectual opposition were to coexist side by side in a peculiar and very Syrian manner with protagonists of the Civil Society Movement taking turns in prison.

There was a time when even parts of the regime seemed to appreciate the constructive and prudent nature of Syria's opposition. Bahjat Suleiman, the feared and powerful former head of Syrian intelligence, wrote in the Lebanese newspaper *al-Safir* in 2003, "In Syria, the regime does not have enemies but 'opponents' whose demands do not go beyond certain political and economic reforms, such as the end of the state of emergency and martial law; the adoption of a law on political parties; and the equitable redistribution of national wealth."[21] Forcible regime change, Suleiman knew, was only on the agenda of select exiles and US politicians.

But instead of reaching out to these opponents, who envisioned a gradual transition toward civil society and pluralism as a soft landing within the system and who shared basic foreign-policy assumptions of the Baathists, the president treated these intellectuals like a gang of criminals in subsequent years. Thus he disillusioned many Syrians who had hoped for a common ground agreement on incremental change. Looking back at Asad's first big opportunity, al-Azm says: "Asad should have brought Riad Seif into a reshuffled government in 2001. His original sin was not to have offered national reconciliation. Many even said that he would have been ready to reconcile with Israel but not with his own people."[22]

With remarkable foresight, Michel Kilo stated in 2003 that the Syrian regime was not reformable. This was true for all authoritarian regimes in the Arab world. "They are not in a situation of stability but in a stable crisis," said Kilo. "When the regime in the Soviet Union wanted to reform itself, the regime was gone. It will happen the same way with the regimes in the Arab world. This is part of the drama of these regimes."[23] Thus, Asad resisted any pressure for real political reform. While others still projected hope in the president, Kilo was without illusions. "Bashar has allied himself with the corrupt forces. Thus he has basically renounced reform. [...] Bashar is not only unable to act, he does not want to act either." The president, he lamented, wanted to circumvent the issue of democracy. "He only wants a reform of power, not of the system." Another leading member of the Civil Society Movement, who preferred to remain anonymous, came to a similar conclusion: "Bashar is aware of his weaknesses." For this reason he is largely keeping out of domestic politics and has abandoned his originally ambitious reform program. "He has capitulated to the hardliners and opted for stability instead of progress."

Suleiman's distinction between opponents and enemies was to become highly topical again in the 2011 upheavals, however, in a much more polarized setting. It is part of the Syrian tragedy that even after the bloody escalation in 2011 some oppositional figures tried to keep the doors open in the hope of dialogue for the sake of Syria's stability and in order to avoid a civil war, most notably Kilo himself. Ignoring the constructive opposition has been one of Asad's gravest errors of his tenure. A decade later, the days were over when obstreperousness was defined as discussion in the back rooms of teahouses suffused with the aromatic smoke of water pipes. The Syrian president learned to face a new and young opposition in the streets and the whiff of gunpowder.

External Shocks Exacerbate the Domestic Situation

The clampdown on the Damascus Spring took place when the young Asad was still in a phase of orientation. External shocks were soon to hit the region and the Syrian regime that were beyond its control. But the Damascus Spring was strangled *before* the first external shocks occurred, which were the terrorist attacks of 11 September 2001 in Washington and New York. After 9/11 and in the "war against terrorism" the Arab autocrats received a new pretext to get tough on oppositional figures (many of whom were located in the Islamist spectrum outside Syria) and a new context in which to frame their policies.

9/11 was a double-edged sword for Damascus. On the one hand, the events opened an opportunity for the Syrian *mukhabarat* to employ their years-long experience in the fight against Islamists of all kinds. Moreover, it represented a point of contact with western interests and was a welcome opportunity to underline the secular credentials of the Baath regime. Indeed, Syria was a valuable partner for the West in the fight against Islamist terrorists. It was no coincidence that the security establishments both in the United States and Israel used to take more conciliatory positions vis-à-vis Damascus than the respective political establishments. For example, George Tenet, who resigned from his position as head of the CIA, was, with his organization, one of the few moderating voices with regard to the Syrian regime within the US administration of George W. Bush.

On the other hand, despite Syria's willing cooperation in the fight against Islamist terrorism, it did not succeed in trading in this commitment for substantially better relations with the United States or

Europe. Such a development would have given a boost to the section of the technocratic and political elite in Damascus that was westward-looking and pragmatic. Some of them lobbied for a rapprochement between Syria and Europe and favoured the signing of the long-postponed EU Association Agreement. One of their key representatives was Sami Khiyami, Asad's economic adviser who later became the Syrian ambassador to London.

The problem for Syria was that two political types of discourses were simultaneously active on the international stage particularly in Washington. One was the discourse oscillating around the fight against Islamist terrorism, which included the debate over direct consequences from the 9/11 attacks. It also went further and posed fundamental questions about a readjustment and the value-orientation of western foreign-policy vis-à-vis so-called pro-Western regimes that had nurtured Islamist terrorism for years, above all Saudi Arabia.[24] If this discourse had been seriously pursued, Syria could have gained strategic advantage on the security level in view of its contribution against militant Islamism (much less, obviously, on the level of democratic governance).

The second discourse had less to do with protecting the United States from terrorist threats but with catering for Israel's security concerns in the region. The pro-Israel discourse did not always overlap with the anti-Islamist-terrorism discourse. In this frame Saddam Hussein's Iraq posed a threat to Israel and thus became a target of the Israel-friendly neo-conservative foreign-policy of the Bush administration. Already at that time also western governments such as France and Germany were not convinced that Iraq had something to do with al-Qaida (and chemical weapons) and opposed an attack on the basis of these reasons.

What it meant for Syria was that the pro-Israel discourse proved stronger and in the end impaired efforts undertaken within the anti-Islamist-terrorism discourse. Because Syria has a political, ideological and territorial problem with Israel, it was never a candidate to enter into a pro-Western camp under the influence of the Bush administration and Israeli interests. Nevertheless, Syria did continue to cooperate with western secret services even after the Anglo-American attack on Iraq up to the fall of 2003. When the regime in Damascus did not harvest any rewards from its engagement, but threats of regime change instead, it was not interested in further cooperation.

This time it was the West that had missed a great chance. Instead of placing Syria within the "extended axis of evil" and of pushing it into the arms of Iran - which many Syrians detest culturally, ideologically and religiously – there was a window of opportunity to focus on common secular values, Syria's tolerance of religious minorities, and on the fight against militant Islamism. Perhaps there was even a chance to embark on technical forms of Syrian-European cooperation such as the Association Agreement. This would have strengthened the pro-western actors within the Syrian bureaucracy and political elite. It would have resonated among parts of the educated middle class as well. Around this time blue car stickers with yellow stars became popular in Damascus that served to imitate EU number plates. Instead, secularist Syria began drifting more and more into the Iranian orbit and into alliances with Islamist groups.

Ideological Encrustation in Context of the Iraq War

The Iraq war was definitely the worst external shock to which the Asad government was exposed. The regime was not ready to embark on democratic experiments as long as its neighbourhood was violent and while the regime's survival was openly put into question by Washington. In turn, this situation represented a comfortable excuse for the regime not to enact any political reforms and to suppress the domestic opposition further.

The Iraq war presented a further opportunity for Asad to demonstrate whether or not he had the political shrewdness of his father. On the one hand, he used the situation very well to galvanize Syrian public opinion and to rally the whole "Arab street" behind him. Asad became a hero from Baghdad to Casablanca as the only Arab leader who confronted a belligerent Bush administration. He even enjoyed the company of European countries like Germany and France in the anti-war camp. It was Syria alone that raised the flag of anti-imperialist pan-Arabism again. The resistance discourse resonated well and Asad enjoyed a time of almost unanimous domestic support. In this matter he could be sure to have great parts of the Syrian opposition behind him. On another note Syria became the hub for Arab resistance fighters who trickled into Iraq. The regime in Damascus was content to get rid of Syrian Islamists who crossed over to Iraq where the Americans even did the job of killing them. Furthermore, the Islamists distracted the Americans from leaving Iraq prematurely and from choosing Damascus as their next target for regime change. An attack on Syria had been a realistic scenario in the first months after the Iraq invasion.

Syria's rejection of military intervention in Iraq was definitely understandable. Raymond Hinnebusch interprets Syria's stance in terms of an ideological rationale: "Opposition to the US was a collective decision that would have been taken by any nationalist leadership in

Damascus. Not only did the invasion threaten vital Syrian interests in Iraq, but it was also an egregious affront to the Arab nationalist values so ingrained in Syrian thinking." After all, the invasion of Iraq was in Israel's best interest.[25]

Against this background of domestic and regional popularity, there is certainly debate as to whether Asad's actions were politically useful in the long run. Discussions with Syrian intellectuals at that time indicated that Asad could have reacted to the Iraq war with more political foresightedness and less ideological fervor. In search of a direction for his foreign policy, Asad used the Anglo-American attack on Syria's neighbor to revive pan-Arab rhetoric. People in tea houses wondered how Hafez al-Asad would have acted in this situation. Some considered the young Asad's policy to be even more ideological than his father's in this respect. For in the end most Syrians were glad that Saddam was overthrown, the Syrian Baathist establishment included.[26] Why should Syria have suddenly lent support to the Iraqi dictator, its Baathist archrival? Michel Kilo is convinced that "Hafez al-Asad would have avoided the conflict with the United States."[27]

It is hard to say whether Asad is really more ideological than his father. He may be less intellectually flexible and less politically shrewd and ready to change sides whenever it looked opportune. The young Asad's ideological hard-line position on the Iraq issue was part of a search for political orientation, a learning process concerning foreign policy rather than an entrenched ideology. It is scarcely surprising that it was the Baath cadres in particular that were said to have advised Bashar to adopt such a strict pro-Iraq and anti-American position. For them it was a welcome opportunity to begin to replenish the empty reservoir of the Baath ideology at a time when they were otherwise running out of answers.

Previously, the best export product Syria had was its foreign policy, as Syrian analyst Samir Altaqi puts it.[28] Hafez al-Asad used it to secure sources of money and room for political maneuver. Syria received money from the Arab states after 1967 because it was engaged in a war with Israel, again in 1973, and once more in 1976 when Syrian troops intervened in the civil war in Lebanon. Then, in 1982, Syria was given support when Israel invaded Lebanon and occupied the southern part of the country. At the same time, Asad secured extensive debt relief from the Soviet Union in exchange for approving the Russian invasion of Afghanistan. In the Gulf War in 1991, Hafez al-Asad did a U-turn and accepted financial aid from the Gulf States, primarily Kuwait, as thanks for supporting the coalition troops against Iraq. Finally, in another U-turn, money flowed from Baghdad after an unexpected honeymoon with the Saddam regime after 1997, and especially after Hafez al-Asad's death.

Applied to the Iraq scenario in 2003 this means that Syria would have naturally rejected the Anglo-American invasion. But the way in which Asad surfed on the wave of anti-Western, pan-Arab nationalism - that notably merged with staunchly Islamist discourses - did not leave much leeway for a future change of tactics. Moreover, this served as a catalyst for Syria to close ranks with Iran, a process that had started with Israel's invasion of Lebanon in 1982. In the wider political scenario the Syrian regime has always been aware of the necessity of US support for any major achievement in the region, if only for the famous last mile in a possible peace agreement with Israel. Many of Asad's foreign policy endeavours after the Iraq war were indeed directed towards finding some kind of acceptance in Washington, hence antagonizing it was impolitic.

After 2011, Syria's foreign policy options narrowed down to alliances with, roughly speaking, Iran, Russia, China and Venezuela. Apparently, family members of higher regime loyalists did not see other options once the uprising began than fleeing to countries such as Malaysia, Iran, the UAE, China, Ghana, and Nigeria.[29] On a political level the newest trend is East Asia, as Syria's foreign minister Walid Muallem announced in anti-Western anger at the end of October 2011 in front of a group of Indian academics and journalists.[30] President Asad underlined this when talking to a Russian TV station. Interestingly, in this interview Asad backdated the decision to look to the Far East to the year 2005, precisely at the moment when an economic reform programme was announced in the Five Year Plan and the European model of Social Market Economy was declared, on paper.[31]

The Unresolved Kurdish Question

Domestically, Asad also missed an important chance during and after the violent Kurdish protests in March 2004, a failure that is likely to close in on him, too. This was one of numerous unresolved problems that cumulatively rebounded on Asad in 2011.

In 2004, bands of Kurdish demonstrators rioted in several cities, including Aleppo and Damascus, setting fire to cars and fighting battles with the security police. But within a week Asad had the situation under control. The riots were sparked during a soccer match but the causes lay deeper. The Syrian Kurds have a score to settle with the Syrian regime. A Syrian population census in 1962 ignored about ninety thousand Kurds in order to stop the demographic balance in the north tilting toward the Arabs' disadvantage. As a countermeasure, the Baath regime tried to settle Arabs in a belt along the Turkish border. An estimated two to three hundred thousand Kurds were without citizenship, including descendants. They were not allowed to travel or to own land, among other things. Today a total of one-and-a-half to two million Kurds live in Syria.

Two aspects are interesting here. First, the moderate opposition from the Civil Society Movement, in particular the human rights lawyer Anwar al-Bunni, tried to mediate and exert a moderating influence on Kurdish activists during the crisis. It was against the patriotism of the Syrian opposition to allow any form of Arab-Kurdish cleavage. Kurdish political leaders who agreed to avoid a rift between them and the Arab oppositional counterparts conceded that they had lost control over parts of their constituency. This would have been yet another opportunity for the regime to reach out to the opposition on behalf of the common national interest in times of external turbulences such as in Iraqi Kurdistan.

Secondly, after the riots Asad travelled to the neglected Kurdish region in northwestern Syria and promised to look into the issue of Kurdish grievances. However, the years passed without any reforms. Rules against Kurds were even tightened, particularly in the field of purchasing property. It was only under the existential threat of the mass protests of 2011 that the president - as one of the first measures - announced a grant of citizenship to stateless elements of the Kurdish population. Thus he intended to prevent a strong Kurdish participation in the protest movements. However, at this point this was no longer received as a welcome reform but considered as a half-hearted concession at the last minute. Thus it lost its political effect like so many other last-minute concessions that Asad announced in the wake of the street riots in spring and summer 2011. The Kurdish issue was one of the easiest concessions to make. Asad lacked the political instinct to launch a solution at the right moment.

Asad's Critical Half-time

During the military intervention in Iraq and the danger this involved for Syria's national security, Asad had the Syrian population staunchly behind him. As mentioned above, anti-Americanism helped to revive the skeleton of Pan-Arabism as an antipode, this time with a more Islamic flavor. The Civil Society Movement simmered after 2003, while economic reforms started to bear initial fruits of visible day-to-day improvement, especially in the banking system.

In this sense the Iraq war as an external shock bore positive potential for Asad. He could have used it once again to strengthen his legitimacy with a popular vote. But he did not. The predicament of reforming without destroying was not resolved. Former and frustrated Baath member Ayman Abdul Nour who has known Asad since his youth said in 2004 in a quite realistic assessment: "If there were free elections controlled by the UN, the president would be sure to win. But if he did this, he would admit that the past thirty years were illegitimate." This is an ideological dead-end. Nour conceded that if there were free parliamentary elections with new parties, the percentage of Baath Party members in parliament would be certain to slide to below 50 percent.[32]

So although Asad as a person continued to have a wide social base - especially within Syria's Alawite, Christian, Druze, and Ismaili minorities as well as the moderate Sunni merchant class - he decided to remain attached to the encrusted Baath structure and within reach of the vested interests of his clan. The role game was well distributed among the leading family members. Asad remained the friendly face to the outside world, his brother Maher and his brother-in-law Asef Shawkat were responsible for the elite soldiers of the presidential guard and the *mukhabarat*, and cousin Rami Makhlouf with his commercial monopolies amassed riches from all kinds of businesses in Syria to secure the clan's finances.

Reference to the "old guard" of functionaries from Hafez al-Asad's times initially served as an argument not to embark on political change beyond administrative adjustments and insulated economic reforms. However, the picture was more complex. Older-aged functionaries were not necessarily part of the "old guard" and young ones not necessarily reformers and westward looking. Gradually, Asad placed his people in the key political and security positions, so that the argument of the "old guard" became less and less tenable.[33] Since mid-2004, observers concluded that Bashar was finally able to consolidate his position within the regime machinery. In July of 2004, he got rid of the long-serving military Chief of Staff Hikmat Shihabi and replaced four-hundred-and-fifty army officers (during the existential threat of the 2011 upheavals, some of these figures were reactivated since Asad was in desperate need of their military experience).

Precisely at this half-time of his rule, when Asad felt relatively secure, he committed one grievous error and missed another formidable chance.

The error was to press for an unconstitutional extension of Lebanon's pro-Syrian President Emile Lahoud at any cost. Asad took a personal decision against the advice of the experienced Vice President Abdul Halim Khaddam and the Baath Regional Command. After the extension of Lahoud's term on 2 September 2004, the UN Security Council, led by a remarkable coalition of the United States and France, passed Resolution 1559. Although it did not name Syria directly, the resolution was a clear challenge to Damascus, calling for the withdrawal of foreign troops from Lebanon, for the disarmament of militias (which meant, above all, Hezbollah), and for free and fair elections the following May.

The insistence on violating Lebanon's constitution and of prolonging Lahoud's presidency bore heavy long-term costs for the Syrian regime. Among other repercussions Syria lost France as a benevolent partner in Europe. It had been France's President Jacques Chirac who was the only western statesman to attend Hafez al-Asad's funeral in June 2000. In subsequent years French consultants poured into Damascus to help Syria to reform its administrative and judicial system. Now it was the personal friendship between Lebanon's Prime Minister Rafiq Hariri and Chirac that proved stronger. Syria was isolated. Not a single Arab state moved a finger in support.

In the following months, the resolution became the main tool for pressuring Syria to withdraw its troops from Lebanon. It also served to considerably narrow Syria's room for political maneuver. Asad had a personal falling-out with Hariri and created an aggressive anti-Hariri atmosphere. So fingers immediately pointed to the regime in Damascus and to Hezbollah after Hariri was assassinated by a huge car bomb in downtown Beirut on 14 February 2005. A wave of anti-Syrian protests swept Lebanon, and Asad had to announce a humiliating withdrawal of Syrian troops from Lebanon. Subsequently, the Special Tribunal for Lebanon, whose role was to investigate the Hariri assassination, became yet another political instrument for Syria's enemies to put pressure on Damascus.

During these months rumours spread of an impending coup d'état in the presidential palace in Damascus. Regime loyalists debated whether Asad was capable at all of defending Syria's national interests. Asad's power became challenged as never before; only in 2011 was a similar discussion again sparked, this time involving much higher stakes. In the Lebanon crisis earlier missed chances began to take their toll. Without having risked a popular vote or at least reached out for national reconciliation with the moderate opposition Asad had nothing much but his clan and the security apparatus to fall back on and piled up political debts to them. This made the president sink ever deeper into the self-interested power structure up to the point of no return. The political blunder of the Hariri assassination, whoever was behind it, marked the beginning of the decline of Asad. The trauma of complete isolation created a certain paranoia also with regard to domestic challenges.

Despite the foreign policy disaster in the beginning of the year 2005 the subsequent months yielded a valuable opportunity for Asad to reposition himself domestically. In June of that year Asad called the 10th Regional Baath Congress, the first one under his leadership. Expectations were high. But oppositional forces and foreign observers were disappointed because they had expected more sweeping political reforms, the end of martial law, immediate permission for the creation of independent parties, reform of the judiciary, and the abolition of the Baath monopoly, as well as the release of the key opposition figures of the Damascus Spring. Instead, the results were merely announcements that never took effect until the regime struggled for survival in 2011.

At the economic level, however, the congress and the five-year-plan under the auspices of Abdulla al-Dardari, Deputy Prime Minister for Economic Affairs, adopted the term Social Market Economy. Dardari was active in opening Syria's economy while trying to limit social shocks. The technocrat gained credibility abroad and with foreign experts who were invited to support the government in this effort, mostly Germans and French. Hopeful signs of economic development blended with worries of an increasing social disequilibrium.

Some progress was achieved between 2005 and 2011. The investment environment was improved. Clearer rules were established and a competition law against monopolies was initiated, be they state owned or private. Import bans were lifted and the state further relinquished its monopoly on imports. Syria had already opened its market by signing the GAFTA (Greater Arab Free Trade Agreement) in 1997, and bilaterally in agreements with Iran, Iraq and, most significantly, Turkey. The Central Bank was granted more autonomy in monetary policies, and a private banking sector was established. A stock exchange was founded and real estate laws relaxed. A sales tax was introduced and older taxes abolished. Foreign debts were comparatively low and foreign money reserves high (more than 60% of GDP). As a result, economic performance improved and foreign investment steadily grew. After Lebanon became more volatile again in 2006 many tourists and investors from the Gulf States went instead to Syria. Tourism boomed. All these positive developments delivered a financial buffer for the government when the Arab Spring revolts paralyzed the Syrian economy. Among other things the government profited from a high amount of foreign currency reserves that it could then use to finance the crackdown.

However, already a few years later it became clear that Asad's government was about to give away a socio-economic opportunity after the country's painful emergence from a socialist command economy. Instead of serious attempts to implement the ambitious concept of a Social Market Economy in a coherent way, economic reforms stopped short at the point where they would have hurt the wider clan's vested interests and privileges. Not even a strategy paper existed that defined a Social Market Economy in the Syrian context.[34]

The dynamics of economic reform had started to fade before the Arab Spring set in. A foreign expert who worked with the government referred to the concept of Social Market Economy at the end of 2010 with the following remark: "I think two or three years ago one was more ambitious than today." Conservative forces realized that their vested political or business interests were in danger if reform got serious, and they started obstructing it. In particular, the Minister of Finance and the Planning Commission were dragging their feet. Apart from that the foreign expert criticized a series of contradicting and technically flawed public policies.[35]

Another foreign expert asked why the Social Market Economy in Syria had one face only, namely Darari himself. It was because thus it was easier to abandon and go on with business as usual whenever necessary without even making the attempt to please western discourses. This is precisely what happened at the beginning of 2011 just before the protests started to gain momentum. Dardari was kicked out of the government.

The chronology is important because it means that this reform concept was meant to fail *before* widespread protests caused the need for pure crisis management. The term Social Market Economy did not find its way into the next five-year-plan, and with the violence that erupted, the Syrian economy and whatever was left of an economic reform process lay in tatters.

The reform announcements of the 10th Baath Congress of 2005, however, had at least served as a yardstick for the opposition's demands. Of particular importance were the party law, the lifting of the state of emergency, and the separation of party and government. The announcement to fight corruption provoked hopes, too, but was not in any case more sincere than the other declarations. For Asad himself the most important outcome of the Baath Congress was a thorough reshuffling of top positions in the National Command and the Central Committee of the party, the government, and the military, consolidating his power.

The Second Wave of Repression

Instead of working toward the fulfilment of the reform promises, a second clampdown on the Syrian Civil Society Movement was soon to follow. In face of the obvious vulnerability of Asad's regime due to the Hariri assassination, the secular opposition gained momentum and was encouraged by western diplomats and politicians. At that time a historic step toward a more unified opposition was achieved through the Damascus Declaration of 16 October 2005. For the first time, all major opposition groups - reaching from the secular Civil Society Movement to Kurdish activists, moderate Muslims, and even the outlawed Muslim Brotherhood in London - issued a broad call for democratic change in Syria. Michel Kilo as the head of the Civil Society Movement composed the original draft before it underwent a lengthy process of discussion among the different groups.

A wave of suppression followed suit in the first half of 2006 when those who had been spared in 2001 were arrested like Kilo and human rights lawyer Anwar al-Bunni. The hunt for signatories of the Damascus Declaration was linked to the accusation of pursuing the agenda of western interests while the Syrian regime suffered from the "Lebanon trauma" of increased isolation and stigmatization. In this respect the suppression of civil society went hand in hand with external developments.

Soon after Kilo was arrested in May 2006 the summer war between Israel and Hezbollah broke out. Its result was a public diplomacy disaster for Israel, although the human and material damage on the Lebanese side was far higher. This war offered Asad yet another opportunity. After Hezbollah declared "victory", Asad in a rather dogmatic speech tried to cash in on the triumph as part as his own policies of resistance against Israel. Syrian public opinion stood behind him, while Hezbollah, and to some extent Asad, became the heroes of the Arab street far beyond the Levant.

In this way Asad could orchestrate the due presidential and parliamentary "elections" in Syria in 2007 with a comfortable cushion of popularity. Syrians were proud of their president who had resisted international sanctions, the US intervention in Iraq and international pressures connected with the Hariri tribunal; he was the only Arab leader left who dared to speak out against Israel. With the main protagonists of the Civil Society Movement behind bars and the street behind him, this would have been another apt moment to formalize his popular support within reformed political structures. Instead, Asad chose to be acclaimed again by manipulated referendum (or "election" as it was officially called) for another seven-year-tenure.

On the public policy level, the selective economic reforms started to hurt the poor and the lower middle classes while corruption and mismanagement thrived. Kilo asserted in late 2010 that transition in Syria toward a post-Baath era was achieved by an alliance of the *mukhabarat* with the new rich.[36]

One aspect of the domestic climate in Syria was that single issue groups with new forms of organization started to replace the old Civil Society Movement as the main actors of change from below. The secular and intellectual civil society activists had pursued a holistic approach of society and politics including conceptions of an ideological *überbau*, did not shy away from delicate issues such as political pluralism and democracy, and posed demands of domestic and foreign-policy relevance.

The new single issue movements did not deal with these dangerous and sometimes unwieldy aspects but focused on immediate priorities such as women's rights, the fight against honour killings or the opposition against the planned reform of the Personal Status Law. As long as they did not mention democracy and did not criticize the President, these local NGOs seemed to enjoy a greater amount of tolerance. Given the practical defeat of the Civil Society Movement by 2010 and the taboo surrounding the notion of civil society, the regime made efforts to re-appropriate the term for itself.

Civil society in Syria – as it became frequently used by the government and international donors and agencies – is not the civil society as understood in the historical context of Europe in the sense of an enlightened, self-determined, critical and politically active *bourgeoisie* or *societé des citoyens*. This is what the Civil Society Movement had in mind when they founded the debating clubs during the Damascus Spring. Accordingly, Kilo defines civil society as "a society of free citizens, exclusively defined by their freedom, independently of any objective ascriptions such as religion or ethnicity."[37]

Syria's First Lady Asma al-Asad put herself at the forefront of "civil society" development in the government's formal sense of "non-government" organizations that work on the grass root level but with clear restrictions. Freedom was clearly not part of this definition of citizenship. In 2007 the First Lady formed an umbrella for the NGOs in

Syria called the Syria Trust for Development. Those civil society activities were given access to shared resources, research and administrative services, and at the same time were restricted to the red lines of the regime because there was no legal activity outside this realm.

This was part of a strategy to enhance the Syrian image abroad by plugging into a widely accepted international discourse. It also served the purpose of repairing distortions of unequal economic development and employing NGOs in a buffer function against socio-economic shocks. Syria Trust was certainly also a tool in the power struggle between conservative ideologues and an attempt by reformists to gain the upper hand and create practical action, looking possibly to incremental change. Finally, it was an attempt to fill the vacuum against potential Islamic charities.

In a bitter irony, considering the clampdown on the Damascus Spring, the Syrian Government's Five Year Plan (2006-2010) addressed the limited role of civil society in Syria's development. Recognizing that "the role of the civil associations and institutions in the socio-economic development wasn't as good as desired," the plan envisaged "radical changes in order to activate and enhance the capabilities of the civil society role in the coming stage." The First Lady conceded in an international civil society conference in Damascus in January 2010: "The government alone cannot move this country forward."[38]

Despite all scepticism this represented an important step forward and a radical change compared to the decades of socialist etatism under Hafez al-Asad in which Syrians had nothing but the state as their reference point in life from charity to education or rural development. Nevertheless, NGO activists hoped for a more liberal NGO law. Since 2005 a new NGO law had been "in planning" but it never materialized similar to the long-awaited law to liberalize the party system that was announced at the 10th Baath Congress.

Observers expressed concern that while covering the conference in January 2010, the Ministry of Information and state press outlets continued to use the term 'paternal society' instead of 'civil society' in their Arabic-language coverage. This, they claimed, signalled that the will to loosen government control over the sector remained limited.[39] The government restricted NGOs mostly to their role in development, shying away from allowing interest groups to play a part in the political system. Given that the economic opening is sandwiched between Baathist state control and neoliberal elements, the Baathist trade unions became frustrated with this development. Even in a market economy, trade unions would have the right to go on strike. Not in Syria.[40]

International Success and the Third Wave of Repression

All in all, the hope that Syria would adopt domestic reforms if it did not continue to feel threatened from abroad did not materialize. In previous years, the thesis was plausible that with Syria's isolation and existential threat against the regime, the political leadership was less ready for experiments and cracked down all the more on opposition movements.

The reversal of this thesis did not come true. Despite a relaxation of international pressure and Syria's re-emergence on the Arab and international stage after 2008, the suppression of political dissenters and human rights defenders even increased. Correlations between domestic and foreign policies that were visible in the past were replaced by contradictions between both realms.

Some three years before the wave of Arab protests reached Syria, the regime in Damascus had started to regain the initiative in foreign policy matters. European governments and even the US administration had come to the conclusion that Syria was at least a stable, politically approachable, and important geo-strategic player in the Middle East whose president was on the path of piecemeal reforms. US President Obama played soft on Syria in his effort to reverse the Syrian drift towards Iran and sent an ambassador to Damascus in January 2011 after nearly six years of diplomatic vacuum. This represented the last foreign policy success for Asad before the popular protests.

It was hard work for the Syrian president to get to this point after years of isolation and stigmatization following the Iraq war and the Hariri disaster. Until 2011 it seemed that Asad had overcome his weakness as a political leader. In light of Iran's post-election Green Revolution in summer 2009 Asad's grip on power looked even stronger than that of his ally President Ahmedinejad. However, two years of successful diplomacy, constructive engagements such as Syria's recognition of Lebanon, rapprochement with Europe and even with the US, and a clever diversification of Syria's foreign policy with Turkey as a close economic and political partner, were destroyed by the failed approach of the Syrian regime towards popular demands.

On the other hand, clinging to power by all means created common grounds with other autocratic Arab states and Asad was able to temporarily ease traditional tensions like those with Saudi Arabia or the Gulf States. It is worth remembering that Syria declared the Saudi military invasion to crush the protests in Bahrain as justified.[41]

However, this overlap of authoritarian interests between Syria and Arab monarchies in the Gulf peninsula was fragile and short-lived.

In all three waves of domestic suppression, the secular Baathist regime silenced above all the moderate, secular voices calling for pluralism and piecemeal reform. In turn, Islamist currents had been gaining ground in Syria. To be sure, the Islamization of opposition politics is a general trend in the Arab Middle East and Syria is not immune. Yet there were other, more specific explanations. First, the regime, despite its secular orientation, and often more out of necessity than enthusiasm, allied with Islamist partners like Iran, Hezbollah and Hamas in an "axis of resistance" to US and Israeli prerogatives. The regime certainly could not afford confrontation on two fronts, external and internal. A second explanation is that, not unlike other Arab regimes, Damascus adopted a conscious strategy of toleration for Islamism. Michel Kilo summarized the division of power between the regime and the Islamists with the pointed words: "Ours is the power, and you get the society."[42] This arrangement could be presented to the West as evidence that Syria would turn Islamist if the Baathists were to lose the state.

In November 2010, when today's events seemed still a remote possibility, Michel Kilo reflected upon the failures of the Civil Society Movement. He complained that the movement had been stopped in its tracks before it was able to broaden its circle of supporters, much less engineer the foundation of parties. But, in accordance with revolutionary patterns in Europe, he said, Syria's educated middle class had been awakened. "Once the spark ignites the younger generation, we can withdraw," Kilo concluded. "At least we have paved the way."[43]

In conclusion, the domestic secular opposition in Syria had not profited from the new dawn in Syria's foreign policy nor had benevolent dissenters or cautioning voices. An experienced Syrian analyst, who worked within the government realm, conceded in an interview in October 2010: "I made the same mistake. I thought there was a correlation between foreign and domestic policy. [...] With or without external pressure we have no political change in Syria. Domestic repression is a continuity not a contradiction."[44]

Analytical voices that had previously been approved by the government were silenced, too. The Orient Center for International Studies (OCIS), a think tank initiated by the foreign ministry and headed by Samir Altaqi, was closed in 2010. Apparently, their analysts became too frank about critical issues, such as economic development and foreign policy, and their contacts with foreigners could have been be misinterpreted as track two diplomacy. A disappointed member of the think tank said that the government was not interested in professional analysis any longer but restricts itself to "intellectual masturbation" within a small circle of its own.[45]

A well-known moderate sheikh, who has held political positions and was known to be pro-regime for years (but who also preferred to remain anonymous here), made a remarkable comment in visible frustration, equally at the end of 2010: "Unfortunately, under the pressure of the US the situation here was better. Now they [the regime] think they have a strong message." He paused and added in a pensive tone: "We are going through a sensitive phase, through difficult times."[46]

These three quotes show that general frustration had been growing visibly within the wider sphere of regime supporters before the upheavals broke out. Barely five months later, the exuberant self-confidence of the Asad regime, the arrogance of power, was seriously challenged. International recognition and importance was a valuable asset that had strengthened the regime's domestic position vis-à-vis the opposition but also vis-à-vis former supporters who had become too outspoken. Every criticism that was directed against Iran was interpreted as a pro-American stance and punished. The room for even cautious dissent had shrunk to dimensions of Hafez al-Asad's times.

The third wave of suppression – and the last one before the uprising in 2011 - started with the arrest of senior human rights advocate Haitham Maleh, head of the Human Rights Association of Syria (HRAS), in October 2009 and had been ongoing since then with various travel bans and the intimidation of intellectuals. The 80-year old Maleh was released only during the hectic weeks of late March 2011, after he had gone on hunger strike. Human rights lawyer Anwar al-Bunni was able to leave prison after ending his regular term in May 2011. Having spent five years in harsh conditions, Bunni stepped into freedom but also, amidst the revolt, into an unrecognizable Syria.

Against this background, the military clampdown during the popular revolt in 2011 has been both a continuation and an escalation of the violation of human rights. Syria was by no means on the way toward serious reforms before the Arab Spring hit the Levant. This happened despite Asad's soft-spoken appearance and Syria's growing recognition on the international stage.

Precisely at the moment when practically nobody in the international community, to some extent not even Israel, really had an interest in Asad's ouster but tried to engage Syria as an important actor in a regional peace scenario, the president committed his most grievous mistakes and missed perhaps the last chances of his political career.

Asad's Last Chances

In its foreign policy, ideological makeup and social composition, Syria differs from Tunisia or Egypt. Yet the reasons and patterns of Syria's crisis are similar to those in other Arab countries. The basic demands are about social justice, the end of arbitrariness and corruption, freedom of speech, perspectives of economic living-conditions, and democracy. Even in highly ideologized Syria the protesters did not go into the streets to blame powers outside their country. They were not linked to an anti-imperialist discourse nor filled with hatred against foreign enemies, not even against Israel. In January one of the first reflexes of the regime in the light of the protests in North Africa was to increase salaries, subsidies and social benefits. The government knew exactly where its soft spot was and reacted quickly. But the measures turned out to be of little use, and were detrimental to the government's long-term reform agenda. Political survival became the first priority.

As in Tunisia, the main protests in Syria were sparked by a rather minor incident. After early peaceful gatherings in Damascus that went nowhere, teens in Daraa sprayed buildings in town with graffiti in mid-March inspired by the Tunisian and Egyptian uprisings. They wrote the famous slogan "The people want to overthrow the regime." Instead of handling this incident with utmost care given the revolutionary environment in the region, the secret police forces arrested the children, put them into prison and tortured them. Family members protested. The police, being unused to civil unrest, used the logic of violence and shot several protesters dead. Anger rose countrywide and triggered more widespread demonstrations, which were met with more brutal force, in turn fueling more protest.

The brutality of the security forces and the brazen arrogance of the governor of the Houran province were inherently typical of a suppressive regime and nothing really remarkable. But in the context of the Arab Spring even the people in Syria had lost their fear. The system failed to adjust its measures accordingly. Authorities lacked a tool set to cope with the situation. The political class was petrified when the protests spread to other towns and regions. It is no surprise that the Arab Spring hit precisely the most suppressive states in the Arab world. Ideologically and structurally, they do not have any room for absorbing societal and political shocks. The mindset as well as the training of authorities at all levels lacks deescalating strategies. In August Asad "acknowledged that some mistakes had been made by the security forces in the initial stages of the unrest and that efforts were under way to prevent their recurrence."[47] By then the damage had already been done.

But for several weeks into the protests it was not yet too late to preserve the famous red line in Syria: criticizing the president. Initially, the demonstrators' wrath did not, by and large, target Asad himself. The fury was first directed toward Bashar's brother Maher, who possesses a reputation for personal cruelty and, as head of the Fourth Division of the Republican Guard, is the backbone of the security solution. Other names increasingly heard in the protesters' chants were Asef Shawkat, husband of Bashar's sister Bushra, and deputy chief of staff of the army, and, above all, Rami Makhlouf, who owns Syria's cell phone companies, duty-free shops and almost everything else that promises quick profits. Like his counterparts in Tunisia and Egypt, Makhlouf is a beneficiary of a classic predatory arrangement. The stories of Makhlouf's corruption incense ordinary Syrians, from the working poor to the hard-pressed middle class. The first wave of protesters in Daraa did not topple statues of Asad but burned down the local outlet of Syriatel, Makhlouf's cell phone company, as well as the court building and the Baath Party offices.

After so many years of stalled reforms and broken promises the president missed this last minute opportunity to convince his population that he was different from the other Arab dictators and that he had the corrupt and violent authorities under control. As a result, he was to lose this crucial last asset, the strong red line that had become intrinsic to Syrian society since Hafez al-Asad. Several times Asad announced that the army would stop the killing of civilians and nothing changed. The positive attributes of his character that had circulated among Syrians throughout these years as well as his authority faded away quickly. Alawi paramilitary units, the so-called *Shabiha*, emerged at the hot spots and added to the indiscriminate slaughter. Either Asad played a double game or he was not in full control. The former confidence that had once been projected by the youngish leader will never be restored again. Asad lost the most important part of his political capital.

In the first weeks of the protests the president mostly kept a low profile, feeding the gossip that he and his family were feuding over how to respond. Asad behaved like the leader of a *"jumlukiyya,"* as the Syrian opposition calls the country's political system, melding the Arabic words for republic and monarchy. Rather than assuming responsibility for the crisis, the republico-monarch shunted blame downward, offering to reshuffle the cabinet and sack the lieutenants responsible for the hot spots around the country. In terms of public relations, the regime tried to make do with sending advisers, deputies or ministers before the cameras to explain its point of view, trotting out the president only in extremis. Much of the regime's verbal response aimed to criminalize the protests or portray them in sectarian terms; in tandem, the regime resorted to lethal force to suppress the agitation.

By playing the sectarian card openly as never before during his rule, Asad destroyed the secular legacy that had been one of the Baathist trademarks. In addition, he tainted the Syrian spirit of tolerance that has century old roots in Syria's social history. In better times the Syrian polity proved much more inclusive than that of other Arab states. The very same regime now chose sectarian strife as its emergency plan for survival. The targeted violence for sectarian purposes has become one of the greatest challenges of the Syrian people: resisting the temptation to fall into this trap.

However, sectarianism can easily become a self-fulfilling prophecy amidst a tremendous propaganda war from all sides. Asad and his government started to criminalize and primordialize oppositional activities in their discourse, and some armed gangs did emerge to fulfill this prophecy, be it with sectarian slogans or with criminal energy. Mistrust between religious groups rose, which cost the protest movement momentum and followers.

Secular Syrians, and especially Alawites, complained about the rising influence of radical Sunni groups, of Saudi influence, and of ever more daring preachers who used their exposure in the only legal civil public spaces – the mosques – to incite an open religious antagonism that had been absent from Syrian streets under the rule of the Asads. Witnesses report that Sunni groups entered Christian villages and intimidated them into joining the protests. In Homs and probably other places as well the *takbir* (the call "allahu akbar" - "God is Great") called from balcony to balcony at nights turned into a battle slogan for some protesters.

All of this frightened religious minorities and secular Sunnis who feared religious radicalism more than a superficial secularist ideology and Baathist authoritarianism, independent from the fact that they despise the regime's violence, too. Many members of religious minorities, such as Christians and the Druze, not to mention Alawis, feared possible retribution from the Sunni majority. High-ranking Christian clerics in Damascus and Aleppo issued statements of support for Asad as late as 2012, fearing an Iraqi scenario.

But cleavages were not so clear cut. Much of the Sunni merchant class stuck to its alliance with the Asad regime. As minorities and middle-class Sunnis make up more than 50 percent of the population, they are not a negligible constituency. This is a highly significant political asset. If Asad lost the moderate Sunni merchant class, he was likely to lose it all.[48] This might happen because of an economic downturn triggered by the protests or a sectarian escalation. On the Christian side some of the community joined the protests in the street, especially at the beginning,[49] and some key oppositional figures are in fact Christians, like Michel Kilo. Christians and secular people met in mosques for the purpose of assembling after Friday prayers. Muslims in Hama invited Christians to join their demonstrations at an early stage, and Muslims and Christians went out to demonstrate harmony as was reported from Damascus to mention a few examples only.

A similar official propaganda that incited sectarian mistrust could be witnessed in Tunisia and especially Egypt, too. However, the peaceful character of the demonstrators and their cross sectarian solidarity prevailed in the minds of the revolutionaries and in the international media (despite some setbacks in the post-revolutionary period). This may be harder to recognize in Syria where for a long time cross-sectarian appeals have had little central direction and few political slogans.

In conclusion, one of Asad's strategies was to keep up the fragile alliance between religious minorities and the moderate Sunni merchant class. This worked as long as the state propaganda managed to uphold a different narrative of the crisis as led by criminals and terrorists directed from abroad. It also worked as long as the clampdown did not pass a certain limit of atrocities and bloodshed. Later it became more and more difficult for clerics, who represent the religious communities, to find supportive words in favour of the regime. The fear of post-revolutionary chaos and possible persecution of Christians or other minorities by radical Islamists as in neighbouring Iraq floated in a delicate balance with disgust about the regime's methods. It was up to Asad and his clan to define the tipping point.

Attempts at Political Appeasement

As the protests escalated further, the regime turned to attempts at political accommodation and, eventually, measures of appeasement. In Tunisia and Egypt, such concessions had no conciliatory effect upon the crowds because the announcements always came a few days or weeks too late. Also in Syria the concessions appeared poorly chosen for the circumstances. On April 7 2011, Asad granted citizenship to 150,000 Kurds in Syria who had been stateless, answering the long-time demand of Kurdish activists. The measure was so overdue that Asad got little credit for it. "Our cause is democracy for the whole of Syria. Citizenship is the right of every Syrian. It is not a favour. It is not the right of anyone to grant," retorted Habib Ibrahim, leader of a major Kurdish party.[50]

Nevertheless, the Kurds did not join the protest movement as vehemently as their deprived status would have suggested. Other reflex-like concessions, like permitting schoolteachers to wear the *niqab* (full face veil) again after abolishing it the year before, closing a casino, and launching a new religious state TV programme were made to placate Islamists, but meant little to the wider base of opposition demonstrators who called for real political reform.

The regime hastily announced political pluralism (or a semblance thereof) under the pressure of the street. Suddenly, long-standing demands of the opposition were readily picked up. Among them in particular was the new party law which was meant to break the monopoly of the Baath Party. The draft had been gathering dust in a presidential desk drawer for years. By Syrian standards, the political concessions were very far-reaching; long years of civil society activism had been unable to achieve them. By the yardstick of the times, however, the moves turned out to be inadequate. The same dynamic holds for the regime's various other promises, like erecting a legal framework for the activities of NGOs or promulgating a new media law. It even holds for declaring an end to martial law, a step that, rhetorically, has always been tied to liberation of the Golan Heights from Israeli occupation and the end to hostilities with Israel. Now it was purely domestic stresses that brought such measures to the forefront of regime calculations. The government was about to lose one trump card after another.

Asad missed the chance to save his legacy by making a last-minute U-turn against internal resistance. After years of waiting he could have promoted himself as part of the solution instead of persisting as part of a growing problem. Many Syrians would have preferred to embark on a transition in stability. For this purpose Asad would have had to overcome his personality and to counter family resistance. Asad did not have the audacity and vision of his personal friend King Juan Carlos of Spain; he was no political hero who would become a champion of reform, instead resisting it within an obsolete and ideologically eroded system. For example, if Riad Seif had been included in Asad's reform government at an early stage in 2011, this would have silenced half of the opposition, opined Sadiq al-Azm.[51] But Asad missed it once again.

Bridges in a Country on Fire

Few leaders who apply a similar cruelty with the aim of suppressing popular demands are as fortunate as Asad with regard to enjoying the last remnants of a moderate opposition. Once again the quote of former head of Syrian intelligence Suleiman from the year 2003 comes to mind: The Syrian regime can be considered lucky that it had opponents but no enemies. This even held true when the country was on fire.

The willingness to build bridges despite all reservations was supported, most prominently, from an unexpected protagonist – Michel Kilo – who has been in conflict with the regime and Asad personally all his life, who was imprisoned twice, and who played a leading role in Syria's Civil Society Movement and the Damascus Spring. In articles in the Lebanese press, Kilo called for a national dialogue with Asad on board. Kilo feared the collapse of Syria's societal fabric and civil war. "This civil/consensual Syrian possibility implies two things", Kilo reflected in the leftist independent newspaper, as-Safir, in April 2011,

> [t]he regime's abstinence from relying on the security related solution in confronting the current situation; and the abstinence of the current movement from calling for ousting the regime. There must be a solution entirely based on a global national dialogue that would push away these two situations in order to prevent the country from turning into a fighting arena [...]. No matter who will be the victorious side, the cost of the confrontation will be deadly for the regime [...]. In addition, [there will also be a hefty price to pay] for the other side, which must realize that erroneous calculations will not lead to the desired freedom but rather to the collapse of the Syrian society's unity in addition to the destruction and dismantlement of the state. The only side that could benefit from a security solution [...] will be Israel.[52]

This discourse once again displays the embeddedness of important parts of the traditional Syrian opposition in the Pan-Arab nationalist discourse.

His stance against the polarizing currents in Syria brought Kilo considerable criticism from oppositional figures who were being hunted down, who had to fear for their lives, who changed their beds every night or who saw their friends being tortured. Others applauded Kilo's far-sightedness in such a crucial moment of Syria's history. Kilo was invited for talks with Asad's adviser Buthaina Sha'ban and Vice President Farouq al-Shara, something that had been unthinkable in the past. Kilo's travel ban was lifted and he went to Europe and Cairo to defend his mission. The German-speaking opposition activist possesses a wide intellectual horizon and knew that he was walking on a dangerous tightrope especially in a situation in which it was not clear where the regime defined its limits of violence. While his method may have been controversial, there is no doubt that Kilo's fundamental goals remained clear. He intended to work toward change "from the status quo to the revolution; from tyranny to freedom; from change driven by the authorities to societal change; and from the familial society to the civil society."[53]

People like Kilo in tandem with the secular editor Louay Hussein and a few others provided another window of opportunity for Asad. Hussein was the main organizer of the famous conference at the Semiramis Hotel in downtown Damascus on 27 June 2011. In the first open gathering of its kind in Syria the domestic opposition tried to redefine itself in heated debates, while an escalation of the conflict was looming on the horizon. Critics said that the regime allowed the meeting with the intention of driving a wedge between the opposition groups inside and outside Syria.[54] The opposition in exile has always rejected anything less than regime change. The declaration of the Semiramis Conference called for a peaceful transition to democracy and an end to the Asad family's 40-year-old monopoly on power. Thus the final goals had become almost identical. What divided the groups were the means on how to get there (apart from personal jealousies and the question of foreign support or even foreign intervention). The Semiramis Conference also called for an immediate end to the security crackdown and the army's withdrawal from towns and villages. This demand has been pending since then without having been fulfilled.

A tweet that was sent out from the hotel gathering attributed the following quote to Michel Kilo: "80 percent of the Syrian population are under 35. Where are they in this conference?" The young people were not interested anymore in declarations and debates. Most of them had never been involved in the discourse of the traditional Civil Society Movement. These young people were now in the streets.

The Semiramis Conference can be considered as yet another last-minute opportunity to engage with the opposition before Syria headed one step further towards the edge of civil war. The minimum condition to continue a dialogue was not met, since the violence continued unabated. Instead, the regime tried to launch a national dialogue on its own. But it failed to convince most oppositional figures inside and outside Syria. A Syrian researcher based in France and linked to the opposition recalled that he received a phone call from Syria's Vice President Farouq al-Shara, who asked him if he would participate in the national dialogue. The researcher wanted to know who the protagonists on the government's side were. Al-Shara responded that it was himself and the President's adviser Bouthaina Sha'ban. The researcher replied that it would not make any sense because even these political veterans did not exert any influence any longer on the Asad clan's decisions. According to the researcher, al-Shara did not even contradict him.[55]

In the standoff between the regime and the opposition Kilo refused to become a member of the Syrian National Council (SNC) that was founded in September/October 2011 and comprises various new opposition groups like the Local Coordination Committees in Syria, long-known protagonists like the exiled Syrian Muslim Brotherhood, other oppositional figures in exile but also members of the domestic opposition like Riad Seif. All of a sudden, Kilo, who had only left prison in summer 2009, found himself on the regime's list as being part of the "good" or the "nationalist opposition" (*mu'arada al-wataniye*) in contrast to the foreign elements of conspiracy against Syria in exile (*mu'arada al-charijiye*) in the regime's terminology.

Whether it is actively promoted by the government or not, the opposition was far from united. Kilo and others formed the Coordination Committee for Democratic Change (CCDC) that stands against the mostly exile dominated SNC. In November several members of the CCDC left the organization because they suspected cooperation between the regime's secret services and the Committee. Syria is polarized not only between pro and anti-Asad camps. The deep rift between the main oppositional streams of thought became tangible when on 10 November 2011 representatives of this Committee, Hassan Abdul-Azim, Michel Kilo, Louay Hussein and Monzer Haloum, were attacked on their way to a meeting with the Arab League on Cairo's Tahrir Square. The Syrian assaulters blamed them for cooperating with the regime in Damascus and called for international protection of civilians in Syria.[56]

The regime's continued and uncompromising "security solution" undermined all persisting efforts to search for a middle way. Moderate oppositional figures who had stood up for a "soft transition" to democracy for a decade were now losing their authority in this polarized environment.

Foreign Initiatives Rebuked and Friends Lost

While the UN Security Council was at loggerheads with Russia and China protecting Syria, the regime did not have to fear any foreign intervention similar to the Libyan case. Nevertheless, several external initiatives tried to build bridges for Asad to end the crisis. All of them were rejected.

The first important opportunity offered itself with the Turkish initiative. In the years after 2004 relations between Syria and Turkey radically improved. Both governments held common cabinet meetings and talked of "family bonds" when they referred to bilateral relations. Not long before the crisis Turkey's Prime Minister Recep Tayyip

Erdogan spent a few days on holiday with the Asad family. The countries abolished visas requirements between the two states and established free trade across their borders. The good relations with Turkey certainly represented the greatest success for Syria in recent years. Damascus had aptly managed to diversify its foreign policy.

However, the uprising in Syria put Turkey's pro-democracy stance to a serious test. After a phase of deliberation, similarly as in the Libyan case, the Turkish government finally opted to support the side of human rights and democracy. Criticism from Ankara rose with the escalation of violence in Syria. Erdogan followed through his role as an advocate of change in the Arab world after harsh criticism against autocrats in Tunisia and Egypt.

Given the former harmony of "family bonds" on the emotional level and the practical improvements between both countries, the visit of Turkey's Foreign Minister Ahmed Davutoglu on 9 August 2011 to Damascus represented a shocking change of paradigm. Davutoglu came to Damascus to deliver an "earnest" message from Erdogan that called for an end to the violence and for all sides to embark on a Turkish sponsored peace plan. Asad reacted indignantly and said: "If you came for a compromise, then we reject it. If you want to have war, then you can have it – in the entire region."[57] This was an affront to Erdogan, not only personally, but also vis-à-vis Erdogan's envisaged role of Turkey as a regional player and mediator.

The willingness to relinquish friends and political trump cards in rage or short-sightedness has deprived the Syrian regime of possible future options within the framework of steering out of the crisis. As mentioned above, the protests hit Syria at a time when Western governments had more or less accommodated themselves with the Syrian regime or at least with its strategic importance in the region despite Syria's tainted human rights record. European and US diplomats, high-ranking politicians, and academics went back and forth to Damascus until the time when the revolt broke out.

Still in late March US Secretary of State Hillary Clinton pointed out: "There's a different leader in Syria now. Many of the members of Congress from both parties who have gone to Syria in recent months have said they believe he's a reformer."[58] This tone was dramatically different not only from the condemnations of the Libyan regime, but also from rhetoric once employed by President George W. Bush. This change of attitude in Washington had been the Syrian political aim for many years. And it was destroyed so quickly.

In July Clinton made clear that the US had definitely changed sides when she claimed that Asad had lost his credibility to rule. "President

Assad is not indispensable, and we have absolutely nothing invested in him remaining in power", Clinton said.[59] In only three months Asad lost yet another important chance to become part of the solution instead remaining part of the problem.

Asad's tone vis-à-vis former friends and the international community became harsher the longer the conflict simmered. He burnt important bridges and lost the soft-spoken and educated image that he had gained in various conversations with foreign heads of state and other politicians. In bilateral conversations as well as in interviews Asad had used to impress his conversational partners with his reflective style.

Despite the rebuke of Turkey's peace offer, Erdogan's hefty criticism against Asad's policies, and the hosting of Syrian opposition groups in Turkey, links between Ankara and Damascus were not immediately cut and economic cooperation continued. Even Davutoglu did not refrain from visting Damascus again in October. But this meeting did not contribute to a settlement either. More menaces emerged from Damascus. According to Arab sources, President Asad said: "If a crazy measure is taken against Damascus, I will need not more than six hours to transfer hundreds of rockets and missiles to the Golan Heights to fire them at Tel Aviv." The Arab source said that the Syrian president told the Turkish Foreign Minister that he would also call on Hezbollah to launch a rocket attack on the Jewish state.[60] Asad's warning came after Davutoglu informed him that he would face a war similar to the NATO aggression on the Libyan regime if he continued to crack down on his people.

After the alienation of Turkey it was up to the Arabs to offer Asad a way out. The Arab League headed by the former transitional foreign minister of Egypt, Nabil al-Arabi, presented two peace initiatives in September and November 2011. Reportedly, Arab states offered asylum to Asad to defuse the situation, too. The mediation attempts included a call to halt all violence against civilians and to withdraw Syrian troops from the cities. The League urged Asad to avoid sectarianism and – entirely in line with the Syrian government – strongly recommended not to create a pretext for any kind of foreign intervention. It further called for compensation for the families of the victims and for a release of all political prisoners. The initiative moreover called on Asad to commit to the political reforms he had announced, including a multi-party system.

Asad chose not to benefit from either of the initiatives, although he formally accepted the second one. But nothing happened, similar to the moment in which he had declared reforms and an end of the shooting in April. Instead, the killing went on also in November and escalated in the cities of Homs and Hama in particular. A refreshed Arab League –

composed of autocracies but also of post-revolutionary states in democratic transition – condemned the killing of civilians in unusually harsh terms. Anti-Syrian Qatar held the presidency of the League, and Syria's adversary Saudi Arabia grew increasingly impatient, too.

Even observers who have often echoed parts of the regime's ideology grew increasingly frustrated by the gambling away of political options. The young historian Sami Moubayed, professor at Syria's prestigious private University of Kalamoon and editor-in-chief of Forward Magazine, reasoned after the failure of the first Arab League initiative: "It could have been a lifejacket for the nation that would end the deadlock between the government and demonstrations which have continued non-stop, despite violence and the rising death toll, since mid-March. By snubbing it, the Syrians probably have lost a golden opportunity." Moubayed recommended: "What they should have done is take it as it stands, then rebrand it as a Syrian initiative - regardless of the Arab League and Qatar - because it is a win-win formula both for the Syrian government and the Syrian street. To quote the *Godfather*, it was an offer they shouldn't have, rather than "couldn't have refused."[61]

In the preceding years Asad had managed to accommodate some of Syria's enemies, including Saudi Arabia, and he had made new friends in the region and on the international stage. Every month that went by in the year 2011 Asad gambled away remnant pieces of his credibility and political leeway. His accumulated foreign policy successes now lie in shatters. He manoeuvred himself into a far worse position than he had been under international isolation following the Iraq war and the Hariri assassination. In case Asad survives the protests, it is improbable that he will ever recover politically and be able to rebuild the foreign policy environment that he had so arduously worked to achieve. He will have to rely ever more on his staunchest ally Iran and on Hezbollah, whereas under his father Hafez al-Asad it was rather Hezbollah that relied on Damascus. If at all, Asad will rule a crippled Syria, domestically and internationally. This is dangerous since the tectonic plates of Iranian and Saudi Arabian interests pass through the Levant. Frictions will increase.

Syria, once the self-confident, pragmatic middle power under Hafez al-Asad and the incarnation of authoritarian stability in the region, could turn into the chessboard of conflicting interests, a hub for arms trade and instability. No matter how events in Syria unfold, it has been shaken beyond return, domestic power structures are shifting, and the regime has destroyed its legacy. Only a peaceful transition could avoid a decomposition of Syria's rich religious and ethnic mosaic and a decline of Syria's weight in the region. After a decade of missed chances and numerous sacrifices Syrians long for the fruits of the Arab Spring: good governance and the end to fear.

---

[1] This chapter is based on Carsten Wieland, Syria: A Decade of Lost Chances: Repression and Revolution from Damascus Spring to Arab Spring, Cune Press, Seattle, 2012.

[2] Carsten Wieland: Syria - Ballots or Bullets? Democracy, Islamism, and Secularism in the Levant, Cune Press, Seattle 2006, p. 40.

[3] Author's interview in Damascus on 23 October 2010.

[4] According to sources in the Civil Society Movement who preferred to remain anonymous; Carsten Wieland: Syria - Ballots or Bullets? Democracy, Islamism, and Secularism in the Levant, Cune Press, Seattle 2006, p. 13.

[5] Moshe Ma'oz: Asad: The Sphinx of Damascus: A Political Biography, London 1988.

[6] SANA, quoted from the English translation.

[7] „Assad könnte zurücktreten", in: *Der Spiegel*, 45/2011 (7 November 2011).

[8] "Bashar al-Assad: the dictator who cannot dictate", James Denselow, guardian.co.uk, 11 May 2011.

[9] Carsten Wieland: Syria - Ballots or Bullets? Democracy, Islamism, and Secularism in the Levant, Cune Press, Seattle 2006, p.13.

[10] Author's interview on 29 October 2011 in Italy.

[11] http://online.wsj.com/article/SB10001424052748703833204576114712%20441122894.html.

[12] http://online.wsj.com/article/SB10001424052748703833204576114712%20441122894.html.

[13] For more on the political history of inter-religious relations in Syria, see Nikolaos van Dam: The Struggle for Power in Syria, London 2011 (4th ed.).

[14] Author's interview in Damascus on 31 October 2010.

[15] A good analysis on the Asad regime's handling of resistance is the piece by Salwa Ismail: Silencing the Voice of Freedom in Syria, in: *Index on Censorship*, 8 July 2011 (www.indexoncensorship.org/2011/07/silencing-the-voice-of-freedom-in-syria).

[16] Quote from Asad's inauguration speech of 18 July 2000: "[...] Thus society will not develop, improve or prosper if it were to depend only on one sect or one party or one group; rather, it has to depend on the work of all citizens in the entire society. That is why I find it absolutely necessary to call upon every single citizen to participate in the process of development and modernization if we are truly honest and serious in attaining the desired results in the very near future."

[17] SANA, quoted from English translation; see also: Alan George: Syria: Neither Bread nor Freedom, London, 2003, p.32.

[18] Interview in the *Syrian Times*, 25 May 2003.

[19] Author's interview in Berlin on 8 July 2011.

[20] Alan George, Syria: Neither Bread nor Freedom, London, 2003, p.170.

[21] *Al-Safir*, 15 March 2003.

[22] Author's interview in Berlin on 15 July 2011.

[23] Author's interview in Damascus on 4 April 2003 and 30 September 2003.

[24] This debate stirred emotions and hit taboos in the United States. In July 2002, Laurent Murawiec, a French neo-conservative who worked in the RAND think tank in Washington, strongly attacked the Saudi connection to international terrorism. In a presentation before the US Defence Policy Board Advisory Committee he called for an "ultimatum to the House of Saud" and described Saudi Arabia the "kernel of evil". When the briefing was leaked, Pentagon and State Department officials distanced themselves from his comments to avert a major diplomatic crisis between the United States and its longtime ally, less than a year after the terrorist attacks of 2001. Murawiec was subsequently expelled from RAND. (See: "Laurent Murawiec, 58; Strategist Said Saudis Backed Terror", in: *Washington Post*, 14 October 2009).

[25] Hinnebusch, Raymond A.: "Syria after the Iraq War: Between the Neo-con Offensive and Internal Reform," *DOI-Focus* No. 14, March 2004, p.12.

[26] International Crisis Group (ICG), Middle East Report No. 23/24: Syria under Bashar, Amman/Brussels, 11 February 2004, Vol. II: Domestic Policy Challenges, p.i.

[27] Author's interview in Damascus on 5 May 2005.

[28] Author's interview in Damascus on 7 May 2004.

[29] According to reports from the oppositional Strategic Research and Communication Center (SRCC) in a briefing from 12 November 2011, "the family members of Asad regime officials have been fleeing the country as over a hundred security, army, and government cars are seen daily at the Aleppo International Airport, with mostly women and children accompanying massive loads of luggage. According to airport employees, most of the passports are Lattakia issued [i.e. with Alawi background], and most of the flights are fully booked departing to Malaysia, Iran, UAE, China, Ghana, and Nigeria."

[30] SANA, 20 October 2011.

[31] "Syria, Russia, India and China are east," Asad said. "There are many countries that have good relations with Syria whether in the east, in Latin America or in Asia. [...] I don't recall any period in which there weren't [*sic*] under some sort of western blockade on Syria, but this blockade intensifies during crises, which is why we decided six years ago – in 2005 – to head towards the east." President Asad to Rossiya 1 TV on 31 October 2011, quoted according to SANA.

[32] Author's interview in Damascus on 16 May 2004.

[33] Over the years, Bashar has managed to place a considerable number of technocrats and personal trustees around himself, some of whom he has promoted to key positions at home and at embassies abroad, such as in Washington or London. A concise overview of such key figures can be found in: Flynt Leverett: Inheriting Syria: Bashar's Trial by Fire, Washington, D.C. 2005, p.71ff.

[34] Samir Seifan: Syria on the Path of Economic Reform, St. Andrew's Papers on Contemporary Syria, Fife 2010, p.12-13, and foreign experts that were interviewed by the author of this article.

[35] Author's interview in Damascus on 01 November 2010.

[36] Author's interview in Damascus on 23 October 2010.

[37] Author's interview in Damascus on 23 October 2010.

[38] "Syrian Civil Society Empowerment 2010: New Directions for Syrian Society", by Stephen Starr, in: *Forward Magazine*, Issue 37, 03 March 2010.
[39] "Access to All Areas?: NGOs in Syria", Dalia Haidar, in: *Syria Today*, March 2010.
[40] There was a minor strike effort during the Diesel price hikes in May 2008. But when two bus drivers had their service taxis confiscated by the secret service, the strike broke down quickly.
[41] "Syria Justifies Saudi Military Intervention in Bahrain", in: *Al-Sharq Al-Awsat*, 20 March 2011.
[42] Author's interview in Kassab on 14 July 2009.
[43] Author's interview in Damascus on 28 October 2010.
[44] Author's interview in Damascus on 23 October 2010.
[45] Author's interview in Damascus on 23 October 2010.
[46] Author's interview in Damascus on 24 October 2010.
[47] "Asad Admits Mistakes", in: *The Daily* Star, 11 August 2011. Statement quoted from a release of India's U.N. mission after a meeting with a delegation from U.N. Security Council members Brazil, India and South Africa.
[48] A good insight into the appropriation of the Sunni merchant class by the old Asad regime can be found in Salwa Ismail: Changing Social Structure, Shifting Alliances and Authoritarianism in Syria, in: Fred Lawson (ed.): *Demystifying Syria*, London 2009.
[49] "Still bubbling: In Syria's third-biggest city people fear for the future", in: *The Economist*, 16 June 2011.
[50] Quoted from Al-Jazeera English service on 8 April 2011 (http://english.aljazeera.net/news/middleeast/2011/04/20114711251531744.html 9).
[51] Author's interview in Berlin on 8 July 2011.
[52] "Yes, there must be a political solution", Michel Kilo, in: *As-Safir*, 16 April 2011, quoted according to Mideast Wire.
[53] Ibid.
[54] By that time the opposition in exile had already had three major meetings in Istanbul (26 April), in Antalya (2 June), and in Brussels (8 June).
[55] Author's interview on 29 October 2011.
[56] "Syrer treffen Arabische Liga", in: *Frankfurter Allgemeine Zeitung*, 10 November 2011.
[57] "Unruhen in Syrien "Wenn Sie Krieg wollen, können Sie ihn haben"", in: *Süddeutsche Zeitung*, 09 August 2011, translated from German.
[58] Hillary Clinton on CBS program "Face the Nation" on March 26, 2011.
[59] www.bloomberg.com/news/2011-07-11/clinton-says-assad-lost-legitimacy-after-mob-attacks-embassy.html.
[60] "Syria: No Message Was Conveyed between Assad, Davutoglu", *Naharnet Newsdesk*, 06 October 2011, http://www.naharnet.com/stories/en/16787-syria-no-message-was-conveyed-between-assad-davutoglu.
[61] Sami Moubayed: "More Missed Chances: An offer Syria shouldn't have refused", *Mideast Views* (http://www.mideastviews.com/print.php?art=547), 21 September 2011.

2
The Syrian Uprising and the Transnational Public Sphere: Transforming the Conflict in Syria[1]
Adam Almqvist

Introduction

> "We're in the process of writing our own version of the Syrian revolution" – Rami Nakhle, Syrian Cyberactivist, Beirut.[2]

> "I am sure you all know that Syria is facing a great conspiracy whose tentacles extend to some nearby countries and far-away countries, with some inside the country" – Syrian President Bashar al-Asad, Speech at the People's Assembly.[3]

> "One man's imagined community is another man's political prison." – Arjun Appadurai, "Disjuncture and Difference in the Global Cultural Economy".[4]

This paper examines the ways in which processes of transnationalism have transformed the nature of the conflict in Syria. Specifically, the analysis surveys the actors (diasporic groups, transnational cyberactivists, cosmopolitan human rights activists), sites (embassies, internet chat-rooms, satellite television newsrooms, Facebook community pages) and strategies (dissemination of narratives, cyberwarfare, symbolic productions) which define, frame, contextualise and mediate the conflict. The analysis is centered on the network of Syrian transnational cyberactivists that emerged amidst the Arab revolutions in Egypt and Tunisia, and their position within the wider oppositional transnational public.

The Syrian uprising is not only situated within the transnational public sphere; it is partly constituted by a struggle over the transnationalization of the public sphere itself. It will be argued that this transnationalization constitutes a central strategy of the global complex of anti-regime actors, referred to here as the oppositional transnational public. Both inside and outside Syria, oppositional political strategies, in addition to efforts to dismantle the material structures of the Baathist state, are geared towards breaking the imaginative hold that the state exercises over people and towards fragmenting its monopoly over representation of reality. This is achieved through the process of transnationalising the domestic public sphere through the configuration of oppositional publics transgressing the national territory, inclusion of diasporas in such publics and the dissemination of revolutionary narratives through transnational media. One of the regime's main tactics, therefore, has been to counteract the transnationalization of the domestic public sphere by reinforcing a strict symbolic dichotomy between "inside" and "outside" in order to re-nationalise and maintain control over the fields of symbolic and discursive production. In addition, it has had to "deterritorialize" its own response by utilizing strategies like cyberwarfare and cracking down on transnational cyberactivists. There is a tendency among scholars and commentators to explore the ways in which transnational processes lead to consolidation of networks, configuration of unified discourses, and popular mobilisation. However, this is often bound up with the Habermasian vision of the public sphere as a monolithic institution which curtails the power of the state. The transnational public sphere, however, is far from monolithic. The consolidation of one transnational public is accompanied by the creation of other publics. When analysing the sites, actors, and strategies that constitute the oppositional transnational public it becomes apparent that this story of consolidation and effective mobilisation runs parallel to processes of fragmentation and polarisation among various transnational publics. This analysis will examine both parallel processes – those of consolidation and fragmentation – and the configurations of power through processes of exclusion and inclusion which underpin such formations.

The paper will demonstrate how the process of the transnationalization /deterritorialization of the public sphere transforms the very nature of the conflict in Syria. The purpose of this investigation is not to explore the dynamics and power struggles between the inside and outside elements of the opposition. Neither does it concern itself with who "owns" the revolution, and whose legitimate and ethical right it is to represent it. Rather it seeks to problematize the distinction between inside and outside and map the contours of various struggles and contestations in the very cleavages between the inside and outside.

Furthermore, it seeks to demonstrate how the practices and strategies of all actors – cyberactivists, local coordination committees, exiled political activists, ordinary protesters inside Syria, the state and regime – are affected by these transnational processes. The research, conducted between May and September 2011, draws on interviews with Syrian cyberactivists, human rights activists and opposition leaders in the US, Canada, UK, Sweden and Qatar, as well as analyses of the online practises of these actors, and covers events during the first six months of the uprising.

New Media and the Transnationalization of the Public Sphere

With the rise of new media in recent decades, scholars from a variety of disciplines have identified a transnationalization of public spheres, and a growing body of literature has mapped the contours of such domains.[5] Transnationalism, here, refers to a process, in the words of Ahiwa Ong, "of disembedding from a set of localized relations in the homeland nation and re-embedding in new overlapping networks that cut across borders".[6] Such networks, while partly embedded in local relations, increasingly migrate to new media. And as Manuel Castells argues, "our society, the network society, organizes its public sphere, more than any other historical form of organization, on the basis of media communication networks."[7]

The increasing transnationalization of the public sphere prompts analyses of political processes disassociated from citizenship and the politics of fixed locations. This de-nationalisation of communicative infrastructures poses challenges to Habermas's initial Westphalian-national model as the correlations between national public spheres and sovereign powers are now eroded.[8] Within these social fields, or transnational public spheres, new forms of political mobilisation, engagement in homeland politics by diasporas, and cyberprotests have emerged.[9] Scholars have also noted how states must transform their power technologies to adapt to this environment, which Basch et al. identify as the "de-territorialized nation states".[10] Diasporas are both products and agents of transnationalization, what Kachig Tölölyan describes as "the exemplary communities of the transnational moment."[11] The transnationalization of the public sphere and new media opens up new channels for diaspora populations to engage with homeland politics.

In Middle Eastern Studies, processes of transnationalism have been studied from a variety of angles: how Arab diasporas use technologies in structuring their relation to the homeland;[12] the formations of new subjectivities online among diasporas;[13] the use of new media in Arab transnational NGOs;[14] the effects of new media on Islam and the consequent fragmentation of religious authority and establishments of alternative sources of religious interpretation.[15] More attention has also been directed in recent years towards public sphere theory in relation to the Middle East, both through new media and more traditional sites.[16] The Arab uprisings present scholars of Middle Eastern Studies and transnationalism with new challenges of how to account both for the way in which transnationalism has eroded regimes' abilities to govern in the first place, and the way in which transnational processes have enabled, not only aided, the revolutionary movements.[17]

Firstly, the paper will historicise the transnationalization of the public sphere in the Syrian uprising by looking at the relationship between the domestic and transnational public spheres prior to the start of the uprising. Secondly, the formation of the oppositional transnational public will be traced by illustrating, through the example of the network of Syrian diaspora cyberactivists, how transnational actors, sites and strategies came to organise into a public. Thirdly, this transnational public will be contextualised within the wider transnational public sphere by looking at the deterritorialization of the state and the processes of inclusion and exclusion which govern the boundaries of the oppositional public.

Origins of the Present Transnationalization of the Public Sphere: Simultaneous Suppression of the Domestic and Opening up of the Transnational Public Spheres in Syria during the 1990s and 2000s

The transnational character of the Syrian uprising can be traced to the parallel incongruous processes of repression of the domestic public sphere and the opening up of the transnational public sphere underway during the last two decades. In the context of Bashar al-Asad's accession to power in 2000, a movement of intense civil society and oppositional activities was set in motion. In his inaugural speech, al-Asad spoke of the need for "constructive thinking", reform and modernisation,[18] and subsequently released 600 political prisoners.[19] Over 1000 civil society activists signed the Statement of 1000, demanding thoroughgoing political reform, and meetings were held among activists and dissidents in private salons. Something approaching a public sphere was shaped as "dissidents at least became aware of each other's existence, and the language of reform was injected into political discourses."[20] This movement, the Damascus Spring, was succeeded by a harsh repression of civil society activism, the Damascus Winter, which exhausted much of the political energy released by the window opened up amidst Bashar al-Asad's succession.

In addition to such political mobilisation, the introduction of the internet provided an instrument for civil society activists to counter the atomisation of society which characterised the regime's power strategies by establishing horizontal relations between new media users and transforming "subjects into citizens".[21] Yet, the regime largely managed to contain this emerging domestic online public sphere. Rather than simply repressing these side-effects across the board, the regime opted for the familiar strategy of what Miriam Cook calls "commissioned criticism", whereby the regime tolerated (occasionally even encouraged) limited dissidence within a set of "red lines" coupled with a capricious policy of repression of those who crossed them.[22] Thus, there was a limited public sphere, configured partly online, yet contained within the regime's orbit of influence through the structures of "red lines". During the Damascus Spring, the Muslim Brotherhood and various secular elements managed to reach some common ground, although they remained fragmented by regional interests, sectarian allegiances, and personal animosity.[23] By 2010, the domestic opposition movement was largely exhausted. Najib Ghadbian, a prominent dissident in exile, described the situation for political dissidence as "desolate."[24]

Parallel to these cycles of mobilisation and repression of a nascent domestic public sphere was an increasing deterritorialization of the wider Arab transnational public sphere. In contrast to the impression given by many accounts of new media and the Arab uprisings, the transnationalization /deterritorialization of the public sphere did not begin with the self-immolation of Mohamed Bouazizi, but can be traced back at least to the 1990s.[25] In the period from the 1960s to the 1980s, television was largely appropriated as a mobilizational tool by Arab states to facilitate state-building and the consolidation of post-colonial nationhood.[26] As the strategies of economic opening and state-domination of informational flows continued in the 1990s, a market was created for satellite channels, such as Al-Jazeera, thus displacing political argument into the transnational public sphere.[27] In response to this development, structural reform of Syria's media landscape was initiated. In 2005, Information Minister Mehdi Dakhlallah declared Syrian newspapers "unreadable" and talked about ushering in a transition from "dirigiste media" to "media with a purpose".[28] The regime decided to allow private print media. Several magazines thereafter emerged, as well as Syria's first private radio channel, *Al-Madina FM*. Ali Farzat, a cartoonist and prominent figure during the uprising, ran a private newspaper in the early 2000s that was closed down after it provoked the censors.[29] While the opening up of the media landscape can partly be read as the regime succumbing to pressures from crony capitalists to open up new markets for private investment,[30] the strategy was a necessary evil for the regime who now competed in an international market for audiences' attention. This process amounted to a loosening of the state's monopoly on dissemination of information, symbols, and over shaping the national imaginary. The relationship between the internet and the regime in Syria prior to the uprising, moreover, must be understood in the context of the contradictions inherent in the regime's modernisation project. Upon his accession to power, Bashar al-Asad, who had been president of the Syrian Computer Society during the 1990s, introduced computer lessons in schools, reduced costs of internet usage and paved the way for the opening of internet cafes.[31] The internet provided an instrument for some people to look beyond Syria and access the increasingly transnationalized Arab public spheres characterised by privatisation of religion, inclusion of diasporas and ideational contestation. In the southern city of Daraa in early March 2011, when 15 school children was arrested and tortured for spraying graffiti on the walls of their schools, the event that sparked mass-demonstrations in Daraa and triggered the nationwide uprising, they did so demanding the "downfall of the regime", a slogan they had picked up via satellite television from the revolutions in Egypt and Tunisia.

These parallel processes described above, of increased ideational contestation in transnational arenas, the suppression of such contestation domestically and the absence of institutions able to incorporate such contestation, was instrumental in precipitating a frontal assault on the hegemony of the state in Syria. This was an assault partly launched from multiple transnational sites by multiple transnational actors utilising transnationalised strategies. This sudden social movement that sprung up in February-March 2011, therefore, cannot simply be understood as a remobilisation of the internal Damascus Declaration opposition, nor an explosive realignment of Syria's nascent public sphere, reinvigorated by revolutionary discourses from Egypt and Tunisia. In addition, it is crucial to take into account Syria's embeddedness within the *transnational* public sphere in order to understand this sudden mobilisation as well as the way in which transnational processes are transforming the nature of the conflict. The Arab uprisings of 2011 in general, and the Syrian uprising in particular, represents a new face in the transnationalization /deterritorialization of the public sphere, a product of the repression of domestic public spheres. Within this transnational public sphere, a dominant oppositional public has emerged in which new actors, sites and strategies have arisen, all of which transcend the physical territory of Syria itself.

Actors: The Anatomy of an Oppositional Transnational Public

Whereas the analysis will primarily focus on the transnational cyberactivists, the wider oppositional transnational public will be sketched out here in order to account for the process whereby the transnationalization of the public sphere becomes bound up with political strategies by various actors in the Syrian uprising and itself becomes a locus of contestation. The Syrian uprising has seen the re-mobilisation of large groups of Syrians based outside Syria. The external oppositional transnational public is a heterogeneous public that is bound together by genealogies of adversity towards the Baathist regime, often tied to their circumstances of migration. Roughly, three networks can be identified which constitute the external segments of the inchoate oppositional transnational public.

One network is comprised by various exiled well-educated cosmopolitan intellectuals and human rights activists that have fled Syria over the last 20 years, usually in relation to civil society activism in Syria, the most prominent of whom are figures such as Radwan Ziadeh, Ammar Abdulhammid and Ausama Monajed. The Damascus winter – the violent crackdown on opposition and civil society movements that had proliferated in the brief period of liberalisation following Bashar al-Asad's accession to power – forced several activists and dissidents into exile, thus inadvertently consolidating such transnational networks.[32] A variety of NGOs,[33] email lists and other communication platforms have linked these actors over the years.[34] At present this group is connected to activists inside Syria and acts as reluctant spokespersons on their behalf.

Another network is made up of the transnational cyberactivists. Due to their opaque methods they have largely been ignored in favour of the traditional opposition's many overt political spectacles. Constituted primarily by younger first-generation immigrants of Syrian descent, this network partly comprises of children of political exiles who fled the country during the turbulent 1980s or later.[35] Also included in this network, which primarily operates online, is a large number of Syrian political refugees who has fled the country during the uprising.[36] The cyberactivists are part of a diasporic elite, often educated in engineering or IT.[37] They are drawn from the loose set of actors who were pioneers in establishing various political, religious and cultural networks among

Arab diapsoras. As Jon Anderson notes in his research on Arab diasporas and new media during the 1990s,

> what sets them apart from other transnational populations is their self-confidence, often manifest as self-righteousness, that is enabled not just by mechanical and electrical technology, but also by the intellectual authority of their professions, and the confidence those inspire, which they apply to -- intrude upon -- other domains, notably of politics, religion and culture.[38]

It is difficult to estimate the number of cyberactivists operating from abroad. According to activists themselves there are hundreds, probably thousands. A minority work openly while others operate under pseudonyms in order to avoid the risk of intimidation by Syrian embassies in host-countries, and to protect their relatives in Syria from retribution.[39]

The third network is the traditional opposition in exile which is comprised of the Muslim Brotherhood, Kurdish Nationalists, tribal leaders and various leftist parties. In the early stages of the uprising, this group of actors saw themselves somewhat marginalised from the wider transnational public. Even though they were formally represented in the Syrian National Council, they lacked influence both on protestors inside Syria and on the wider oppositional transnational public. There is a generational divide in the oppositional transnational public which has proved hard for the traditional opposition to overcome.[40] It is clear, as Joe Pace has noted, that the ideology of the old-guard opposition did not resonate among young people and there have been complaints that they "were stuck in the 1960s, bogged down in the mire of petty ideological debates over the fine points of Leninism, socialism, or Nasserism".[41] Another factor is the sites at which the oppositional transnational public operates. Osama Kadi, a Canada based intellectual and dissident says that "traditional political parties have not adjusted themselves to the new era of technology. This has created a gap between themselves and the street".[42]

Thus, whereas there has been significant disparity between the external traditional opposition, such as the SNC, and the protest movement inside Syria, other external oppositional networks, such as the cyberactivists, have been embedded in networks consisting of inside and outside actors which transgress the national territory of Syria. However, even if the liberal, inclusivist discourses of the cyberactivists and diaspora intellectuals dominated the oppositional transnational public in the early stages, underpinning this partial ostracization of the traditional opposition, there were ample indications that the ethnic (Kurdish nationalists), sectarian (Muslim Brotherhood), tribal (various tribal leaders) and ideological (various leftists parties) ideational affiliations were gaining more influence as the uprising expanded and incorporated new sets of internal and external actors, and as the regime violence led to a radicalization of the conflict.

With the revolutions in Egypt and Tunisia as a backdrop, these three amorphous networks started to mould into a transnational public, by shaping networks among themselves and with protestors and activists inside Syria, as well as parts of the diaspora which has more or less enthusiastically participated in online discussions on the platforms established by these core activist networks

In the early stages of the uprising, the cyberactivists were particularly instrumental, especially in their efforts to bridge the wider Arab uprisings and Syrian politics. Inspired by the Tunisian and Egyptian revolutions, groups of young, computer-savvy, people from the Syrian diaspora – scattered all around the globe, from Beirut and Paris to Los Angeles and Stockholm – began to assemble online with the aim of instigating a similar trajectory for Syria. A Facebook page labelled *Syrian Revolution 2011* was set up to provide a virtual platform for oppositional activism. By early February it amassed around 17,000 followers, the overwhelming majority of whom were from the diaspora. They called for an Egyptian-style "day of rage" in Damascus on the 8th of February. Only a negligible amount of people turned up, all of whom were swiftly dispersed by security police. But despite the initial failure, in time the network interweaved itself through new media with local activists and came to perform certain crucial functions in an activist networks that stretches far beyond the borders of Syria.

Throughout the first weeks of the uprising, some of the main webpages, operated primarily by diaspora cyberactivists, were instrumental in running the day-to-day operations of the uprising. Fiddaalidin Al-Sayed Issa, a Sweden-based activist and one of the main players behind the Facebook site *Syrian Revolution 2011*, said in May 2011 that "we guide young people down there. When we called for a Friday demonstration, people take to the streets - everyone follows. We determine the dates of the demonstrations with the help of people on the ground."[43] Local activists in Syria have since become better organized. Local Coordination Committees, first formed in Daraa, quickly spread to Homs where the organisation has been the most accomplished.[44] As the uprising wore on, the transnational cyberactivists, who constitute one network within the oppositional transnational public, gradually adopted a more supportive role of mediating and representing the revolution.

Concurrently, various exiled intellectuals and human rights activists acted as spokespersons for the revolution and as the point of call for international media, NGOs and foreign governments. These actors were unconstrained by the very circumstances – repression, immobility, communication difficulties – which have forced the internal networks to remain organic and leaderless. Moreover, they hold positions in society which have granted them certain authority. As one young cyberactivist commented, "I cannot walk into Hillary Clinton's office. I wouldn't be taken seriously. We need these people [who] act as representatives of the revolution".[45] Many of the intellectuals became reluctant spokespersons, not hesitant in their commitment to the revolution, but uncomfortable appearing to represent a movement which they had neither instigated nor controlled.

Another development – in addition to the shift in responsibilities from outside to inside in the day-to-day running of the protests – has been a simultaneous increased professionalization and division of labour in the cyberactivist networks. They are now divided into smaller units, each with a designated set of tasks. Some sort through the enormous amount of incoming information and images which can range between 1000-5000 messages per day. If the information or images originate from a secure source, they are immediately published on the main webpages (which include *Syrian Revolution 2011*). If not, they must be verified by local trusted sources. Other teams deal directly with the international media, responding to questions, facilitating contacts between foreign journalists and local activists, and writing press releases. Moreover, some groups directed hacker attacks towards the Syrian Ministry of Defence and against the website of the first lady Asma al-Asad, among other targets.[46] Fearing an Egypt-style internet closure, activists also smuggled in around 100 satellite phones, modems, cameras and laptops during the early stages of the uprising.[47]

Many activists emphasize trust as important in solidifying networks. For example, in these circles, not being able to return to the homeland signifies both their genealogies of activism and their level of commitment. A core network was established among those who were active from the start, before the revolution got underway, and who have been able to build relationships across borders.[48] Abdulsattar Attar, an activist based in Belgium, notes that "every one of these activists knows two or three trustworthy sources in different towns and villages across the country. In all, we're in contact with thousands of Syrians."[49] By delegating enormous amounts of cumbersome work, they offloaded a huge number of tasks from local activists, who can then focus on other activities. Thus, in all these ways – division of labour, professionalization, and the consolidation and building of trust – a network of transnational cyberactivists was configured online and offline which was instrumental in supporting the uprising during the early stages in a variety of ways.[50]

Sites: Syrian Revolution 2011

The oppositional transnational public operate on multiple sites in and out of cyberspace, including blogs, Skype, Facebook community sites, discussion fields on various websites, chatrooms etc. One example will be taken up here: the Facebook website *Syrian Revolution 2011*. The site which had by September 2011 amassed over 300,000 followers was the centrepiece of the Syrian transnational cyberactivists.[51] Activists themselves claim that the website was visited over 11 million times every day. In May 2011, it was estimated that the site's users were comprised of about 35% Syrian nationals residing in Syria, 50% from the Syrian diaspora around the world while the remaining 15% were mainly other Arabs in other Arab countries, figures illustrating the immense presence of the diaspora in the virtual anti-regime spaces.[52] The Facebook page was run by around 20-25 operators with 400 activists in the wider support-network, 100-150 of whom are from the diaspora. In the early stages of the uprising, the statements it produced several times a day effectively translated into semi-official policy for the revolution. At present, the site is only one among hundreds that have sprung up since the uprising started. In addition to *Syrian Revolution 2011* (hereafter: SR2011) there are the Local Coordination Committees of Syria, Shaam News Networks, Syrian Days of Rage, The Syrian Activists' Network, With You Syria, to name a few, and a cohort of websites which represents local towns and villages throughout Syria.[53]

On the SR2011 Facebook website, administrators, most of whom are from the diaspora, churn out statements, often accompanied with videos, sometimes at a rate of one every second minute. The statements range from logistical information for protesters and reports of ongoing demonstrations to quotes from articles and grand political declarations in the name of the revolution. In the comments field beneath each announcement, individuals from the 300,000-strong pool of followers (or just anyone with a Facebook account) opine, discuss and reflect over the administrators' statements, roughly at a rate of 30-100 comments on each statement. Users can also choose to "like" the statement, expressing their approval of a statement's content. Between 100 and 400 members "like" each statement.

The administrators on *SR2011* practise special terms of usage. It is strictly forbidden to incite violence, attack individuals or to use "inappropriate language". Failure to abide by these rules can result in expulsion from the site. On March 24th a "code of ethics against sectarianism in Syria" was released, in an attempt to prevent revolutionary discourse being tainted by sectarian rhetoric. Intense discussions took place over how to take the revolution forward and the site for the most part practised interactivity and inclusivity. Before each Friday, a poll was held over what the Friday-protests should be called. They often carried slogans with political purposes: for example, one Friday protest was called Azzadi – the Kurdish word for "Freedom" – in an attempt to reach out to the Kurdish community.

Sites within the transnational public sphere, such as SR2011, very much function as public spheres in the Habermasian sense. They fulfil the institutional criteria: open access, bracketing of identities (whereby location, education, social status and gender are almost always concealed), and discussions based on issues pertaining to common affairs of all Syrians. But, despite the cyberactivists' insistence that they simply mediate neutral information they are fed from people "on the ground", statements are given meaning in relation to the particular context in which it is expressed, and *Syrian Revolution 2011* has not been immune to charges of carrying sectarian or other exclusivist undertones. The latter part of the paper will explore these processes of inclusion and exclusion which govern the borders of the oppositional transnational public.

Strategies: Narratives of the Revolution and the Struggle for Representation

As the uprising has progressed, the most central task of the oppositional transnational public has been to project certain narratives of the revolution to both Syrians and the outside world. In much of the scholarship on Syria in recent decades there has been a general consensus that the Syrian regime has not ruled by an ideological mandate, but rather operated purely on the basis of coercion and neo-patrimonialism.[54] However, a few scholars – most notably Lisa Wedeen and Miriam Cook – have illustrated that the workings of Syrian authoritarianism have been more complex and have entered the ideational realm in subtle ways through disciplinary power and the production of knowledge by the regime.[55] As Charles Tripp observes of Middle Eastern states, power functions as an "imaginative construct, shaping ideas of community, and the means whereby collective identities can be protected, and interests furthered".[56] Therefore, internally, activism in the oppositional transnational public is as much about breaking the imaginative hold that the state exercises over people and fragmenting its monopoly over representation of reality as it is about dismantling the material structures of the Baathist state. Externally, it is about breaking the isolation of the country, exposing injustices, and shattering the lingering image of Bashar al-Asad as a reformer. In this twin pursuit, representing, writing, capturing, and mediating the revolution and constructing it publically to internal and external actors become powerful techniques, and these are activities in which the transnational public has been integral, if not wholly dominant. This is part of a strategy to transnationalize the public sphere and, by doing this, break the regime's hold over the internal symbolic sphere.

The production and dissemination of narratives of the revolution have largely been accomplished through the projection of imagery. There is a belief among activists that imagery escapes the inherent bias of regular news reporting. Radwan Ziadeh, a liberal intellectual based in Washington, argues that "if the Egyptian revolution was the Facebook revolution, the Syrian revolution is the Youtube revolution". Ziadeh sees a risk that the revolution, due to the lack of access of international media inside Syria, will become a revolution in numbers – number of people killed, detained, missing – whereas "personal stories" are being overlooked.[57] The oppositional transnational public's task is to provide the context – through stories, real people, images – that provides meaning to such factual statements.

Crucially, these narratives reach their audience principally through satellite television rather than through social networking. Even though the regime lifted its Facebook ban in mid-February 2011 in a bid to appease growing discontent, sites such as *Syrian Revolution 2011* are banned and have to be accessed by circumventing firewalls through proxy-servers, a practise in which activists have developed great sophistication.[58] Moreover, internet connection speed has been slow to the extent of making the use of Facebook and Youtube "virtually impossible".[59] In 2008, only 16.8% of Syrians had access to the internet, compared for example to 48.5% in Iran. A more reliable channel of reaching a Syrian audience is indirectly through satellite-channels such as Al-Jazeera and Al-Arabiya which broadcasts images published by the main opposition websites. The "Al-Jazeera effect" is often overlooked in contemporary debates on the role of new media in the Arab revolts in favour of the more *in vogue* "Facebook effect" and "Youtube effects"; yet, the satellite channels magnify discourses that emanate from the internet platforms by feeding them into their own narratives.

Whereas the Syrian uprising received little attention in Al-Jazeera's broadcasting during its early stages, it has since firmly been placed in the "Al-Jazeera narrative" of the people against the dictators.[60] As Mark Lynch has noted,

> Events do not speak for themselves. For them to have political meaning they need to be interpreted, placed into a particular context and imbued with significance. Arabs collectively understood these events quite␣quickly as part of a broader Arab narrative of reform and popular protest ---the "Al Jazeera narrative" of an Arab public challenging authoritarian Arab regimes and U.S. foreign policy alike.[61]

This demonstrates the salience of not divorcing the internet from its wider position within the transnational public sphere. The internet, of course, has different qualities in that it constitutes a public sphere in itself because of its many-to-many communication. But satellite TV-channels have been wholly dependent on information and images from actors inside Syria, the so-called "citizen-journalism" (which is in the Syrian uprising more akin to activist-journalism). Disseminating information and images has become an integral part of the whole oppositional transnational public, much of whose networking is geared towards these tasks. It is not only about illuminating their strategies "on the ground", but constitutes a strategy in itself. Without these media outlets being willing to mediate stories from inside Syria, the internet would be reduced to a logistical network for core activists and a public sphere for members of the Syrian diaspora.

In an upscale neighbourhood in Cairo, renowned British-Syrian activist Rami Jarrah has set up a media centre along with a number of Syrian activists, with the primary aim of influencing media coverage on Syria. The organization, which is called Activists News Association (ANA), is partly funded by western NGOs but claims to be politically independent.[62] The media centre issues daily reports of events in Syria which is distributed to international media organizations. According to Jarrah, "a lot of the time, news reports are basically copy and paste from our reports".[63] Moreover, the Cairo media centre distributes easy-to-use flip cameras to activists inside Syria and offers media training to improve the quality of citizen journalism. One aim is to get quality footage of demonstrations, especially to provide a counterweight to the dominance of footage of violent clashes, "without someone screaming Allahu Akbar in the background", which is then distributed to news media.[64] The centre is also setting up a radio station which will first broadcast online with the future aim to establish terrestrial radio inside

Syria. The ANA Cairo media centre is a palpable example of the strategies deployed by actors within the oppositional transnational public. Such strategies are located in the fissures between the inside and the outside and aim to transnationalize the domestic public sphere. ANA's audience consists of both Syrians inside and outside Syria as well as a wider international audience. It aims to play an active role by asserting its agency in how the conflict is portrayed, thus challenging both regime narratives and international media narratives. It helps disseminates discourses that all actors – inside and outside – need to relate to. Actors within the oppositional transnational public have not been immune from accusations of taking advantage of the ambiguous informational environment that surrounds the conflict. The internal environment in Syria is characterized by the absence of foreign media and independent observers. The oppositions' narrative constructions have led to charges that the image of the revolution has been tweaked in order to make it more palatable to western audiences. It has been claimed, for example, that the role of women is exaggerated and communal strife played down.[65] Another example is the case of Zainab al-Husni who was reported have been brutally killed in detention and, through the story's diffusion by Al-Jazeera, Amnesty International and the BBC, quickly became a martyr. Al-Husni later appeared on state television, apparently unharmed.[66] Moreover, mystery surrounded an "intelligence document" which was published on one of the main websites, allegedly outlining the details of the state's plans for a brutal crackdown on dissent. Questions have been raised over its authenticity, which has proven impossible to verify.[67]

When analyzing these processes of narrative construction, it is important to emphasise the contingencies inherent in the formation of transnational publics. The way in which new media have been conceptualised in the "Arab Spring", as facilitating the rise of a counterhegemonic public sphere, very much reflects the one-dimensional view of the public sphere envisioned by Habermas. Walter Armbrust has situated such concern within the "'the mania for newness'" which is "structured, implicitly, by an old and familiar concern for politics that structures much of Middle Eastern Studies ... to construct a democratic public sphere or undermine it."[68] A transnational public is not, by definition, counterhegemonic and subversive, but can itself inhabit power which may generate new forms of resistance.[69] Building on Gramsci, Fraser claims that "the official public sphere, then, was – indeed, is – the prime institutional site for the construction of the consent that defines the new, hegemonic mode of domination"[70] Thus it is important not to test practices against the predetermined linear trajectory towards democracy and inclusivity but to be attuned to the contingencies that govern these trajectories in the formation of transnational publics. While the oppositional transnational public have been remarkably successful in their media operations, and while the new media has facilitated this dissemination, it is important to emphasise the ways in which these operations are bound up with specific political strategies located in their effort to transnationalize the public sphere.

Mutual Transformations of the Transnational and the Local

When examining transnational processes in relation to the Syrian uprising, the "outside" can never be detached from the "inside". Transnational publics transgress physical space and the local and the transnational – the "inside" and the "outside" – are mutually transformed in the process. Such intertwinement is partly inherent in the medium of the internet, which, as Saskia Sassen notes, is a technology that "is partly embedded in actual societal structures and power dynamics: its topography weaves in and out of non-electronic space".[71] Consequently, the local and the global become increasingly intertwined in a process Roland Robertson has called "glocalization".[72]

In the case of Syria, part of the transnationalization of the public sphere is the incorporation of both external and internal actors – protestors on the street, activists etc. – within it. As Guidry et al. states in their survey on the transnational public sphere:

> One should attend to the variety of ways in which social movements enter the transnational public space, are potentially transformed by the encounter, and perhaps even influence globalizations themselves. That is to say, the transnational public sphere renders the global and local mutually transformative. Social movements as a whole – their objects, participants, leaders, and analysts – are all part of this process.[73]

The transnationalization of the public sphere described above engenders a global gaze under which protests are performed. In this sense, the protests are part of a performativity which stages them according to specific political strategies informed by the discourses of resistance on the one hand and directed towards national and transnational audiences on the other. Therefore, events "on the ground" are not only reflected neutrally to the outside world via new media; this gaze fundamentally transforms the strategies of protestors in the first place, an example of how the local and the transnational become mutually transformative.

One such specific strategy is the use of so called "flying demonstrations", a type of flash protest whereby people gather at a predetermined location for a very short period of time, just long enough to film the demonstrations, only to disperse again, thus avoiding a response from the security police.[74] Videos are then disseminated, often via transnational cyberactivists, to various news networks. Another way in which this transnational gaze alters the strategies is the overt political messages displayed at demonstrations. When Russia and China vetoed tougher sanctions against the Asad regime in the UN Security Council, for example, protestors trampled on large Russian and Chinese flags in an act of overt defiance.[75] Journalist Nir Rosen, moreover, observes an instance in Ramel, a neighbourhood in Latakia, where a big screen was set up during a protest showing Al-Jazeera's live footage of demonstrations all around Syria. When the screen turned to the Ramel crowd, "the crowd went wild, jumping, clapping and shouting, singing loudly in unison, shooting more fireworks into the air".[76] Online and offline practises, external and internal strategies, are all intertwined. An organisation, the Syrian Non-Violence Movement, which promotes civil disobedience, distributed small packages in the streets of Syria with Facebook messages from the online forums.[77] On twitter, activists have launched the #EyesonSyria campaign to maintain the transnational gaze. Thus, the transnationalization of the public sphere transforms and appropriates all actors involved in the Syrian uprising, including the state, to which we will now turn.

The Deterritorialization of the Syrian state

The Syrian uprising, by unleashing multiple communicative capacities, represents a forceful transnationalization of Syrian politics, a process resisted by the regime and those loyal to it. The response has manifested itself both in the ideational realm, by casting the oppositional transnational public as a conspiracy and by reinforcing the distinction between the "inside" and the "outside", as well as by targeted measures, such as cracking down on dissidents abroad and launching various kinds of cyberwarfare. The regime, although occasionally hapless in dealing with the new media, has demonstrated awareness in dealing with the transnationalization of the public sphere, which it recognises as a potent, if not existential, threat. One strategy is to cast itself as the subject of a grand conspiracy partly manifested in "media wars" and "virtual wars". In his first speech after the uprising began, Bashar Al-Asad said:

> And I am sure you all know that Syria is facing a great conspiracy whose tentacles extend to some nearby countries and far-away countries, with some inside the country. This conspiracy depends, in its timing not in its form, on what is happening in other Arab countries […]
>
> Some satellite T.V. stations actually spoke about attacking certain buildings an hour before they were actually attacked. How did they know that? Do they read the future? This happened more than once. Then, things started to become clearer. They will say that we believe in the conspiracy theory. In fact there is no conspiracy theory. There is a conspiracy […]
>
> In the beginning they started with incitement, many weeks before trouble started in Syria. They used the satellite T.V. stations and the internet but did not achieve anything. And then, using sedition, started to produce fake information, voices, images, etc. they forged everything.
>
> It is a virtual war…They want us to incur a virtual defeat but using different methods.[78]

Counterrevolutionaries have a clear presence on the internet, although they are not as coherent and sophisticated as the oppositional transnational public. Mirroring the regime's discursive tactics, several regime-loyal actors on the net have elaborated on the alleged conspiracy. Websites have sprung up that seek to uncover "the plot against Syria". On these sites, one of which is called 'TrashSyria', the extent of such a plot is laid out in a conspiratorial manner linking famous transnational cyberactivists, such as Fiddaldin Issa and Rami Nakhle, to regime critics such as Abdulhalim Khaddam, the former Vice President, and Michel Kilo, a veteran Christian dissident.[79] Even more astounding are the claims that the plot is spearheaded by a random cohort of disparate Jewish and/or American actors such as AIPAC, US diplomat Jeffery Feltman, and the French philosopher Bernard Henri-Levy. On the TrashSyria website, users can choose to virtually 'spit on', 'mark as toxic waste' or 'dump' the Syrian activists, dissidents, and opposition leaders whose profiles are displayed on the site, mirroring the often disturbingly unsavoury rhetoric of the regime.

Another strategy designed to counteract the oppositional transnational public is the emphasis regime discourse put on the dichotomy between "inside" and "outside". Bashar Al-Asad makes this distinction very clear:

The first (group) constitute a part of our national component and all of the demands I heard from them were raised underneath the national umbrella. They had no foreign agenda and no foreign connections. They were against any foreign intervention under any pretext, asking to engage, however, rather than be marginalized. They wanted justice [...]
The latter are a small group. It is true that they made an impact; they tried to manipulate others. They tried to manipulate the good majority of the Syrian people in order to achieve different purposes. Differentiating between the two groups is very important [...]
There are people who are well paid to carry out video cameras, film and collaborate with the media...They distorted the country's image in the outside world and opened the way, and even called for, foreign intervention.[80]

Producing and maintaining the appearance of a distinction is itself a mechanism that generates resources of power. But the state has also directed direct attacks against sites and actors who constitute the oppositional transnational pubic. One weapon used is the Syrian Electronic Army (SEA). This group is closely connected to, if not directly instigated by, the regime. Information Warfare Monitor, a research institute at the Munk School of Global Affairs, University of Toronto, found that the SEA's website was registered by the Syrian Computer Society and its servers hosted by a branch of the same organisation. This is the same computer society that was headed by Bashar al-Asad during the 1990s and founded by his brother Bassel al-Asad.[81] President al-Asad himself mentioned the Syrian Electronic Army in his 3rd speech after the start of the uprising on the 20th of June 2011.[82] Its purpose is to attack websites that spread news hostile to the Syrian regime and to combat "the fabrication of the facts of events in Syria".[83] The SEA has used so-called defacement, stripping a website of its content and replacing it with political messages, and spamming attacks. One instrument that it uses is the so-called Denial of Service tools, designed specifically to obstruct certain users from accessing the websites of Al-Jazeera, Al-Arabiya, BBC News, and Orient TV, a Syrian satellite broadcaster.[84]

A second tactic has been to use the regime's network of embassies and other regime-loyal actors to suppress dissidents abroad. Fiddaaldin Issa, a cyberactivist, noted that "as an activist, I have had many problems with the regime. They have named me on television several times, they say that I'm no longer a Syrian, that I have betrayed my country. They have phoned me and sent letters saying that they know where I live, what my wife and my son's names are."[85] Such stories are not uncommon. Sometimes the security services clamp down on net activists abroad by forcing detained protestors inside Syria to open their Facebook accounts and reveal their network of friends.[86] Threatening messages are then sent to cyberactivists around the world.

During a protest in Paris on the 26th of August, several demonstrators were attacked by a group of nine men, several of whom had diplomatic passports according to French police.[87] Amnesty International also recounts the case of Malek Jandali, a Syrian-American composer who performed at an anti-regime rally in Washington. Four days later his parents were violently assaulted by security agents in their homes in Damascus.[88] The list goes on and on. In October 2011, a Syrian-born American, Mohamad Soueid, was charged with spying on US activists who oppose the Damascus government. According to the indictment, Soueid, who had allegedly met president al-Asad in June 2011, sent 20 video and audio recordings of protests in the US to the mukhabaraat between April and June 2011.[89] Throughout North America and Europe these activities have been widespread.

This demonstrates how the transnationalization of the public sphere, a strategy pushed by the oppositional transnational public, has been counteracted by the state and elements loyal to it. Even if these tactics are harsh and disturbing, it is too simplistic to proclaim, as some commentators have, this struggle to be a battle of "light vs. darkness, openness vs. secrecy, transparency vs. anonymity, and old media vs. new media."[90] What is certain, however, is that these processes have led to a fragmentation and polarisation which has left many Syrians, inside and outside of the country, to reject both the regime and the oppositional transnational public.

Fragmentation in the Transnational Public Sphere: Exclusion and Inclusion

The formation of the current opposition has led to a transnationalization of the public sphere, in which Syrians can debate topics unthinkable only a year ago. Sites such as *Syrian Revolution 2011* practise Habermasian "rational" forms of debate, and inclusivity and openness are the norm. Through the complex network of narrative dissemination, the regime's stranglehold on the symbolic sphere and the informational environment has been broken. However, the opposition had by the end of 2011 failed to reach a critical mass and to sway what is commonly labelled the "silent majority". Activists and opposition members make sense of this failure in two ways. One is by pointing towards the fear factor, the harsh repression by the security services. The other way is by invoking a kind of false consciousness logic, arguing that people are deluded by the regime's propaganda machine. Ayman Abdel Nour, editor in chief of the All4Syria news website, sums up this view: "we have a silent majority that does not know the truth, and even if they try to know they will reject the truth out of fear".[91]

While the new media offers sites for the formation and consolidation of imagined communities, such an arena, with its inherent multi-polarity, also lends itself to fragmentation of imagined communities. This goes for both inside and outside Syria. Journalist Anthony Shadid notes that "in Alawite villages, only government television is watched. To do so in Sunni neighborhoods amounts to treason. There, Al Jazeera and Al Arabiya are the stations of choice."[92] For a long time, the monied classes in Aleppo and Damascus, moreover, are able to live in oblivion to what is going on in the country.[93] Internet forums and chat sites are awash with Youtube videos showing either pro-government demonstrations in Damascus or oppositional protests, usually from Homs or Hama, supposedly reinforcing their argument about what is "actually" going on in Syria. The bracketing of identities, moreover, may lead to, what Jon Anderson calls a lack of "civility in the vernacular", which further polarises public opinion.[94]

As has been shown, the activist networks within the oppositional transnational public have been successful in promoting their narratives of revolution, which have locked into the 'Al-Jazeera narrative' of Arab peoples against repressive dictators. But the binary nature of this narrative runs the risk of excluding more ambiguous and ambivalent interpretations of the conflict. In the process large segments of Syrians – inside and outside of the country –who do not share the fervour of the revolutionaries have felt excluded.

By operating through new media rather than in real life situations, the oppositional transnational public can act unitarily as a public. New media also facilitate non-hierarchical organisations which mobilise people around an abstract idea rather than, for example, a charismatic leader. The opposition has been strongest when disembedded from "real" space. International pressure to organise formally – culminating in the formation of the Syrian National Council – undermines the appeal to universal values that have underpinned the wider oppositional transnational public by reifying such values in individuals and groups which embody certain sectarian, political and other identities. The often sincere efforts by the oppositional transnational public to reach out to various communities have been undermined by the broader process of fragmentation and polarisation evident in the transnational public sphere. Thus the transnationalization of the public sphere, and the state's efforts to counteract it, polarise public opinion and fragment imagined communities. In between remain nuances, grey zones often labelled 'the silent majority', which constitute a variety of Syrians, inside and outside Syria, who are mobilised by neither of these discourses.

All actors involved – the state, the opposition, the cyberactivists – are part of such fragmentation. The new media landscape, which partly constitutes the transnational public sphere – its inherent plurality, many-to-many characteristics, and user-generated content (even in the case of satellite television) – facilitates such fragmentation. It is now easier than ever to operate in distinct, yet coherent, information and ideational environments. As Guidry et al. argues:

> The coherence of a common public sphere that invites multiple publics to participate is, however, a difficult concept to grasp. Without the unity afforded by the nation it appears nearly impossible. The symbol of the nation and the ideology of national self-interest enables a common public sphere within nation-states to be imaginable. A postmodern sensibility of difference undermines the ease with which the communality of that national public sphere can be imagined. It is even more difficult to imagine a *transnational* public sphere that has no global imaginary uniting the variety of publics constituting it.[95]

Thus, the transnationalization of the public sphere undermines the kind of "reading together" that Benedict Anderson identified as integral in the formation of imagined communities, and by extension, nation-states.[96] It follows naturally, then, that the transnationalization of the public sphere itself is a political strategy by the oppositional transnational public, one that the state tries to counteract.

Conclusion

This paper has traced the formation of an oppositional transnational public within the transnational public sphere where dichotomies of offline and online, and inside and outside are blurred. Whereas there has been a gap between the external formal opposition, such as the SNC, and protesters inside Syria, other external oppositional networks, such as the cyberactivists, have been embedded in networks consisting of inside and outside actors thus transgressing the national territory of Syria. In the Syrian uprising, processes of transnationalism render the strategies of the local and the transnational mutually transformed. Within the oppositional transnational public, new sets of actors, sites and strategies overlap with protestors and activists inside Syria. In a struggle located in the realm of representation, narratives of the revolution have successfully been disseminated through sophisticated networks of activists which transcend national boundaries. In response, the regime has had to deterritorialize the state in order to deal with the threats posed by the transnational strategies of the oppositional public. The transnational public sphere does not function as a unitary public sphere as Habermas envisioned. Instead, it reflects – as well as underpins – in a dialectical process, a fragmentation and polarisation, of transnational publics rooted in imagined communities. The inclusivity, debates over common concern, and status bracketing practised within the oppositional transnational public are predicated on *a priori* processes of inclusion and exclusion – contingent on attitudes toward the uprising – that make such coherence possible in the first place.

Thus, in times of turmoil, like the present one in Syria, the struggle over transnationalization provides the backdrop against which formerly stable identities are set in flux, configurations of power and influence are renegotiated and imagined communities reimagined. The transnationalization of the public sphere has redrawn patterns of identity and belonging. Whereas these spaces go a long way towards transcending established boundaries between class, gender, social status, political allegiance and sects, they are strictly ordered according to a new binary of regime supporters and critics.

---

[1] The author would like to thank Christa Salamandra and Eric Hooglund, who read and commented on earlier drafts of this paper.

[2] Rami Nakhle, "Syria's cyber revolution – video", *The Guardian*, (April 26, 2011). http://www.guardian.co.uk/world/video/2011/apr/26/syria-internet-protest [accessed September 10, 2011].

[3] Syrian Arab News Agency, President al-Assad Delivers Speech at People's Assembly, *SANA*, (March 10, 2011) http://www.sana.sy/eng/21/2011/03/30/pr-339334.htm [accessed October 12, 2011].

[4] Arjun Appadurai, "Disjuncture and Difference in the Global Cultural Economy", in *Modernity at Large: Cultural Dimensions of Globalization* (Minneapolis: University of Minnesota Press, 1996). p.32.

[5] Appadurai, *Modernity at Large*; Thomas Olesen, "Transnational Publics: New Spaces of Social Movement Activism and the Problem of Global Long-Sightedness, *Current Sociology*, Vol. 53. No. 3. (May 2005). pp. 419-440; Steven Vertovec, "Conceiving and researching transnationalism", *Ethnic and Racial Studies*, Vol. 22, Issue. 2 (1999). pp. 447-462.

[6] Aihwa Ong, "CYBERPUBLICS AND DIASPORA POLITICS AMONG TRANSNATIONAL CHINESE", *Interventions* (March 2003) Vol. 5, Issue. 1, pp. 82-100. p. 87.

[7] Manuel Castells, "The New Public Sphere: Global Civil Society, Communication Networks, and Global Governance" *The ANNALS of the American Academy of Political and Social Science*, Vol. 616, No. 1 (March 2008). pp. 78-93. p. 79.

[8] Nancy Fraser, "Transnationalizing the Public Sphere: On the Legitimacy and Efficacy of Public Opinion in a Post-Westphalian World", *Theory Culture Society* Vol. 24 No. 7 (July 2007). pp. 7-30. Jürgen Habermas, in his seminal study, *The Structural Transformation of the Public Sphere,* argued that a public sphere, where private people come together as a public, emerged in the coffeehouses and saloons in Great Britain, France, and German between 1680 and 1730. These spheres were, according to Habermas, characterized by open access, the bracketing of identities, rational debate, and the concern with the affairs of the public as a whole (Habermas 1989; Calhoun 1992). These sites were arenas for critical discussions and, through a kind of "reading together" that Benedict Anderson (2006) has singled out as crucial in the formation of "imagined communities", such arenas constituted a public sphere.

[9] Kyra Landzelius (ed.), *Native on the Net: Indigenous Cyber-activism and Virtual Diasporas over the World Wide* Web (London: Routledge, 1999); Wim Van De Donk, Brian Loader & Dieter Rucht (eds.), *Cyberprotest: New Media, Citizens and Social Movements* (London: Routledge, 2003); Lynn A. Staeheli, Valerie Ledwith, Meghann Ormond, Katie Reed, Amy Sumpter & Daniel Trudeau, "Immigration, the internet, and spaces of politics", *Political Geography* 21 (2002): pp. 989–1012.

[10] Linda Basch, Nina Glick Schiller & Crista Szanton-Blanc, *Nations Unbound: Transnational Projects, Postcolonial Predicaments and Deterritorialized Nation-States* (London and New York: Routledge, 1994).

[11] Kachig Tölölyan, "Rethinking Diaspora(s): Stateless Power in the Transnational Moment", *Diaspora: A Journal of Transnational Studies*, Vol. 5, No. 1 (Spring 1996), pp. 3-36. p. 5. Diasporas, moreover, are often in the forefront of communication technological advancements because of the difficulties involved in reaching their audience. See Karim H. Karim, *The Media of Diaspora* (London and New York: Routledge, 2003).

[12] Khalil Rinnawi, "'Cybernaut' Diaspora: Arab Diaspora in Germany", in Andoni Alonso & Pedro G. Oiarzaba (eds.) *Diasporas in a New Media Age: Identity, Politics, and Community* (Nevada: University of Nevada Press, 2010), pp. 265-290.

[13] Matthijs Van Den Bos & Liza Nell, "Territorial bounds to virtual space: transnational online and offline networks of Iranian and Turkish-Kurdish immigrants in the Netherlands", *Global Networks*, Vol. 6, Issue: 2 (2006) pp.201-220; Mark Graham & Shahram Khosravi "Reordering Public and Private in Iranian Cyberspace: Identity, Politics and Mobilization", *Identities: Global Studies in Culture and Power*, Vol. 9, No. 2 (January 2002). pp. 219-246.

[14] Caroline Nagel & Lynn Staeheli, "ICT and geographies of British Arab and Arab American activism", *Global Networks* Vol. 10, Issue 2 (April 2010). pp. 262–281.

[15] Dale Eickelman and Jon Anderson, *New Media in the Muslim World: The Emerging Public Sphere* (Bloomington: Indiana University Press, 2003); Steven Vertovec, "Diaspora, Transnationalism and Islam: Sites of Change and Modes of Research" in Stefano Allievi & Jørgen Nielsen (eds.) *Muslim Networks and Transnational Communities in and across Europe* (Leiden, Boston: Brill, 2003);

Pete Mandaville, *Transnational Muslim Politics: Reimagining the Umma* (London: Routledge, 2001).

[16] Mark Lynch, *Voices of the New Arab Public* (New York: Columbia University Press, 2006); Dale Eickelman & Armando Salvatore (eds.), *Public Islam and the Common Good* (Leiden: Brill, 2006); Lisa Wedeen, *Peripheral Visions: Publics, Power, and Performance in Yemen* (Chicago: University of Chicago Press, 2008); Muhammad Ibrahim Ayish, *The new Arab public sphere* (Berlin: Frank and Timme, 2008).

[17] The primary theme covered hitherto in debates pertaining to transnationalism and the Arab uprisings is new media, and information and communications technologies (ICTs). Opinions range from the notion that new media have created counterhegemonic public spheres (Cottle 2011), to the idea that its significance has been marginal at best (Gladwell 2011). By far the most prominent interpretation, among activists and scholars alike, however, has been to conceptualise new media as merely a mobilisation tool that channels discontent external to the media itself (Kamis and Vaughn 2011; Zuckerman 2011). Arguably, new media in the Syrian uprising carries both less and more weight than a mobilisation tool. It carries less weight in the sense that its power to mobilise people is often overemphasized. But it also carries more weight. If evading the technology fetishisation and distinct lack of historicisation of which these debates often suffer, one may attend to the various ways that new media have facilitated a deterritorialization and transnationalisation of the public sphere, of which the Arab uprisings only represents a new face, and conceptualise it as a powerful instrument in breaking the monopoly of representation of reality enjoyed by many Arab states and with it, their ability to govern their respective territories and nations.

[18] President Bashar al-Asad's Address to the People's Council, 17 July 2000, in Alan George, *Syria: Neither Bread Nor Freedom* (London: Zed Books, 2003). p. 32.

[19] Najib Ghadbian, "Contesting Authoritarianism: Opposition Activism under Bashar Asad" (forthcoming).

[20] Joshua Landis & Joe Pace, "The Syrian Opposition", *The Washington Quarterly*, Vol. 30, No.1 (Winter 2006-2007). pp. 45-68. p. 48.

[21] Roschanack Shaery-Eisenlohr, "From Subjects to Citizens? Civil Society and the Internet in Syria", *Middle East Critique*, Vol. 20, issue. 2, (2011) pp. 127-138.

[22] Miriam Cooke, *Dissident Syria: Making Oppositional Arts Official* (Durham and London: Duke University Press, 2007); Lisa Wedeen also notes a similar tendency which she labels "licensed criticism". Lisa Wedeen, *Ambiguities of Domination: Politics, Rhetoric, and Symbols in Contemporary Syria* (Chicago: University of Chicago Press, 1999).

[23] Ghadbian, "Contesting Authoritarianism".

[24] Ibid. p. 21.

[25] Before that, other media, such as cassettes, print media and radio, had altered the political landscape in the Arab world in various ways. New Media, indeed, must be seen, as Armburst notes, as "part of a long history of adaptations of mass media rather than as merely a tool of opposition". Walter

Armburst "New Media and Old Agendas: The Internet in the Middle East and Middle Eastern Studies", *International Journal of Middle East Studies*, Vol. 39, Issue 4. (October 2007): 531-533. p. 533.

[26] Lila Abu-Lughod, *Dramas of Nationhood: The Politics of Television in Egypt* (Chicago: University of Chicago Presss, 2005).

[27] Lynch, *Voices of the New Arab Public*, pp.38-40.

[28] Marwan Kraidy, "Syria: Media Reform and Its Limitations, *Arab Reform Bulletin*, Vol.4, issue 4 (May 2006), no page numbers.

[29] George Weyman "Empowering Youth or Reshaping Compliance? Star Magazine, Symbolic Production, and Competing Visions of Shabab in Syria", M.Phil Thesis in Modern Middle Eastern Studies (Wadham College, University of Oxford, 2006) p.13. Ali Farzat was brutally beaten by security police during the uprising.

[30] Private media are often run by businessmen close to the regime. Even Rami Makhlouf, the arch-crony capitalist, has a financial interest in the "independent" TV station *Al Dunya*.

[31] Shaery-Eisenlohr, "From Subjects to Citizens?", p. 129.

[32] Joshua Landis & Joe Pace, "The Syrian Opposition: The Struggle for Unity and Relevance, 2003-2008" in Fred H. Lawson (ed.) *Demystifying Syria* (London: SAQI and Middle East institute SOAS, 2009). p.132.

[33] For example, Thawra Foundation, Movement for Justice and Development in Syria, and Damascus Center for Human Rights.

[34] Osama Kadi, author's interview (04 August 2011).

[35] Whereas little is known about the status of the children of political exiles, Human Rights Watch reported in 2000 that children of Syrian political exiles whose parents were recorded on black lists in Damascus, could not obtain Syrian passports, nor be entered in Syria's civil status register, thus depriving these children of their legal nationalities. Immigration and Refugee Board of Canada, "Jordan/Syria: Ability of the Muslim Brotherhood to obtain passports for its members and friend", (30 October 2000), http://www.unhcr.org/refworld/docid/3df4bed2c.html [accessed 5 October 2011].

[36] Perhaps the most well-known is Rami Nakhle who has frequently featured in international media from his hide-out in Beirut. See Hugh Macleod and Annasofie Flamand, "Tweeting the police state", *Al-Jazeera*, (9 April 2011) http://www.aljazeera.com/indepth/features/2011/04/20114814358353452.html [accessed 14 August].

[37] As one activist told me, apart from discussions regarding their work in assisting the uprisings, the most common topic discussed in these circles are exams and university life. Yasir al-Sayeed Issa, author's interview (16 August 2011).

[38] Jon W. Anderson, "Cybernauts of the Arab Diaspora: Electronic Mediation in Transnational Cultural Identities", prepared for Couch-Stone Symposium, POSTMODERN CULTURE, GLOBAL CAPITALISM AND DEMOCRATIC ACTION, University of Maryland (10-12 April 1997). Available at

http://www.naba.org.uk/CONTENT/articles/Diaspora/cybernauts_of_the_arab_diaspora.htm. [accessed 13 August 2011].

[39] Practices of intimidation of expatriates and retribution on relatives in Syria have been widespread, according to reports. C.f. Jay Solomon & Nour Malas "Syria Threatens Dissidents Around Globe, U.S. Says", Wall street Journal, (17th August 2011) http://online.wsj.com/article/SB10001424053111904823804576504260399843094.html [accessed 6 August 2011]; Richard Hall, "Syrian embassy in 'intimidation' row", *The Independent* (29 June 2011) http://www.independent.co.uk/news/uk/politics/syrian-embassy-in-intimidation-row-2304123.html [accessed 6 August 2011]; *Amnesty International Report*, "The Long Reach Of The Mukhabaraat: Violence And Harassment Against Syrians Abroad And Their Relatives Back Home" (London: Amnesty International Publications, 2011), http://www.amnesty.org/en/library/asset/MDE24/057/2011/en/31e11754-c369-4f17-8956-548b2f7e1766/mde2405720 11en.pdf [accessed 11 October 2011].

[40] At the Antalya opposition conference in May-June 2011, the young-old divide was apparent. Mohja Khaf, a prominent poet and activist based in the US, tweeted from the conference: "[The] younger generation that is carrying this rev[olution]: don't care ab[ou]t old lines of diff[erence]s: Ikhwan, secularists". See Mohja Kahf, Live-Tweet from Antalya Conference, Twitter, https://twitter.com/#!/ProfKahf [accessed 25th July]. According to other reports, youth meetings were held in harmonious fashion, while the traditional opposition squabbled over the wording of the final declaration. See Hussain Abdul-Hussai, "Youth shine at Syrian Antalya conference", *Lebanon Now*, (1 June 2011) http://www.nowlebanon.com/NewsArchiveDetails.aspx?ID=277162 [accessed 1 Aug 2011].

[41] Joe Pace, "A Better Way to Protect Civil Society in Syria", *Syria Comment*, 22 February 2006.

[42] Osama Kadi, author's interview (04 August 2011).

[43] Fiddaalidin Al-Sayed Issa. Author's interview, interview Published in *Syria Comment*, "Syria Revolution 2011 facebook page Administrator, Fidaaldin Al-Sayed Issa, Interviewed by Adam Almqvist" http://www.joshualandis.com/blog/?p=9705&cp=all.

[44] Anthony Shadid, "Coalition of Factions From the Streets Fuels a New Opposition in Syria", *New York Times*, (30th June 2011) http://www.nytimes.com/2011/07/01/world/middleeast/01syria.html?pagewanted=all [accessed 8 August 2011].

[45] Yasir Al-Sayeed Issa, author's interview (16 August 2011).

[46] The group, which calls itself "Anonymous", have used so called "defacements", replacing the content on these websites with political messages. On the Syrian Ministry of Defense website, the following message was displayed: "To the Syrian people: The world stands with you against the brutal regime of Bashar al-Assad. Know that time and history are on your side - tyrants use violence because they have nothing else, and the more violent they are, the more fragile they become... - Anonymous.". As reported by "Zee" on *thenextweb* (8 August 2011), http://thenextweb.com/me/2011/08/08/anonymous-

reportedly-hacks-syrian-ministry-of-defense-website/_[accessed 10 September 2011].

[47] Author's interviews; Anthony Shadid "Exiles Shaping World's Image of Syria Revolt", *New York Times*, (23 April 2011) http://www.nytimes.com/2011/04/24/world/middleeast/24beirut.html?pagewanted=all [accessed 28 July].

[48] It should also be noted here, in passing, that many of the transnational cyberactivists have strong relations to net-activists from Egypt that may have helped to set up networks.

[49] As reported by Perrine Mouterde, "Syria's growing army of young, media-savvy activists", *france24*, (09/08/2011) http://www.france24.com/en/20110809-syria-growing-army-young-media-savvy-activists-social-organising-internet-online [accessed 25 August 2011].

[50] Since this research was conducted in the summer and fall of 2011, the three externally based networks – intellectuals and human rights activists, cyberactivists, and the traditional opposition – have continued to weave together in different ways. This process has been contingent on new actors entering the scene and the new directions which the uprising has taken. Some young cyberactivists have been incorporated in the formal bodies claiming to represent the revolution, such as the SNC, while others, especially among those recently exiled, have been demobilized by what is perceived as a corrupt, undemocratic and Islamist-dominated external opposition. Some elements of the traditional opposition, such as the Muslim Brotherhood, have taken on a more prominent role. Meanwhile, the efforts to arm the rebel groups have meant that an economy of violence has sprung up which interweaves with elements of the oppositional transnational public. Several prominent Syrian businessmen, some of whom were expatriates prior to the uprising and some of whom had been based in Syria and loyal to the regime, have become nodes in the oppositional transnational public as the flow of funds has become increasingly important. The oppositional transnational public, meanwhile, has been reinforced by the continued flow of refugees from Syria, further blurring the boundaries of inside and outside while local oppositional groups are being formed in places which have seen a large influx of refugees, such as Cairo.

[51] The site does not have closed membership but is open to anyone with a Facebook account to use. The 300.000 + followers are people who have chosen to "like" the site.

[52] Fiddaalidin Issa, author's interview (15 May 2011). The heavy presence of the diaspora on these spaces reflects the huge discrepancy of access to the internet in Syria compared to the countries where the diaspora are residing. These figures are likely to reflect the discrepancy in the level of internet usage in Syria compared to the host-countries of the diaspora. Syria has internet usage rate of 19.8% of the population compared to 77.3% and 82.5% in the US and UK respectively. Statistics from (10 June 2011) http://www.internetworldstats.com [accessed 4 October 2011].

[53] Local Coordination Committees http://www.lccsyria.org/en/; Shaam News Network http://www.facebook.com/ShaamNewsNetwork; Syrian Day of Rage http://www.facebook.com/SyrianDayOfRage; The Syrian Activists'

Network http://www.facebook.com/SyrianActivistsNetwork; With You Syria http://withyousyria.com/.

[54] C.f. Volker Perthes, *The Political Economy of Syria under Asad*, (London: I.B. Tauris, 1995); and Alan George, *Syria: Neither Bread nor Freedom* (London: Zed Books, 2003). For example, Perthes argues that "the regime does not...prescribe what people should believe" (Perthes 1995: 189). According to George, the state is "deploying its habitual brute force rather than coherent argument" – it is "power for its own sake" (George, 2003: ix, xxi).

[55] Wedeen, "Ambiguities of Domination"; Cooke, "Dissident Syria"; George Weyman, "Empowering Youth or Reshaping Compliance? Star Magazine, Symbolic Production, and Competing Visions of Shabab in Syria" M.Phil Thesis in Modern Middle Eastern Studies, Wadham College, University of Oxford, (2006). Available at http://users.ox.ac.uk/~metheses/WeymanThesis.htm.

[56] Charles Tripp, "State, Elites and the 'Management of Change" in ed. Hasan Hakimian & Ziba Moshaver (eds.) *The State and Global Change: The Political Economy of Transition in the Middle East and North Africa* (London: Curzon, 2001) pp. 211–31. p. 219.

[57] Radwan Ziadeh, author's interview, 8th Aug 2011.

[58] It is not uncommon among activists to interpret the lifting of the Facebook in the light of the heavy presence in the early stages of the uprising of actors loyal to the regime. It is conceivable, therefore, that the state planned to continue the practice of commissioned criticism, by relying on its ability to control the cybersphere.

[59] International Crises Group, "Popular Protests in North Africa and the Middle East (VII): The Syrian Regime's Slow-motion Suicide", East/North Africa Report N°109, (13 July 2011). p.19.

[60] Michael Young, "The shameful Arab silence on Syria", *The Daily Star* (7th April 2011) www.dailystar.com.lb/Opinion/Columnist/Apr/07/The-shameful-Arab-silence-on-Syria.ashx#axzz1JmRDT2au [accessed 10 October 2011]. In this regard, many analysts have pointed to the close relation enjoyed by Bashar al-Asad with the Qatari Emir Sheikh Hamad bin Khalifa al-Thani. Yet, Sheik Hamad reportedly felt rebuffed by Mr Asad after the uprising commenced in Syria. See Anthony Shadid, "Qatar Wields an Outsize Influence in Arab Politics", *New York Times* (14 November 2011)www.nytimes.com/2011/11/15/world/middleeast/qatar-presses-decisive-shift-in-arab-politics.html [accessed 15 November 2011].

[61] Mark Lynch, "Tunisia and the New Arab Media Space", *Foreign Policy* (15 January 2011) http://lynch.foreignpolicy.com/posts/2011/01/15/tunisia_and_the_new_arab_media_space [accessed 8 August 2011].

This demonstrates the importance of not analysing the internet in isolation from broader communication strategies. As illustrated above, much of the diasporic mobilisation on the internet is geared towards disseminating these narratives into the wider media sphere.

[62] http://www.facebook.com/ActivistsNewsAssociation.

[63] Rami Jarrah, author's interview, Cairo 27 March 2012.

[64] Rami Jarrah, author's interview, Cairo 4 October 2012.
[65] International Crises Group, "Popular Protests in North Africa and the Middle East (VII): The Syrian Regime's Slow-motion Suicide", East/North Africa Report N°109, (13 July 2011). p. 2.
[66] Ian Black and Matthew Weaver, "Syria attacks 'media fabrications' by showing 'beheaded' woman alive on TV", The Guardian (5 October 2011) http://www.guardian.co.uk/world/2011/oct/05/syria-attack-media-beheaded-girl [1st November].
[67] Michael Isikoff, "A Syrian plan to attack protesters?" *MSNBC* (April 13, 2011) http://www.msnbc.msn.com/id/42578969/ns/world_news-mideast_n_africa/t/syrian-plan-attack-protesters/#.Tse9mEOF9tM [accessed August 16, 2011]; Questions Surrounding the Syrian Counterprotest Plan, *Stratfor: Global Intelligence* (April, 15 2011).
[68] Walter Armburst "New Media and Old Agendas: The Internet in the Middle East and Middle Eastern Studies", *International Journal of Middle East Studies*, Vol. 39, Issue 4 (October 2007). pp. 531-533. p. 532. As some commentators have pointed out, there is a latent orientalism in the new media determinism of some western commentator (for instance, in labeling the Tunisian as the "Twitter Revolution"), a sense in which the docile "Arab Street" could not rise up against repression without western technological influences. For such critique, see Luke Allnutt, "Tunisia: Can We Please Stop Talking About 'Twitter Revolutions'?" *Radio Free Europe/Radio Liberty* (15 January 2011), http://www.rferl.org/content/tunisia_can_we_please_stop_talking_about_twitter_revolutions/2277052.html [accessed 10 August]; Tarak Barkawi, "Ritual in the revolution?" *Al-Jazeera Opinion* (6 October 2011) http://www.aljazeera.com/indepth/opinion/2011/10/2011105124250607722.html [accessed 7 October 2011]. Barkawi notes: "Not only is their agency erased by the hype over ICTs, but what they fought for - political participation - also is assumed to be somehow 'Western'."
[69] As Kathryn Mitchell argues, transnational pockets of subaltern counterpublics have systematically been conceptualised as spaces of subversion. Katharyne Mitchell, "Different Diasporas and the Hype of Hybridity", *Environment and Planning D: Society and Space* Vol. 15, Issue. 5, (1997) pp. 533-553.
[70] Fraser, "Rethinking the Public Sphere". p. 62.
[71] Saskia Sassen, "Digital networks and power", in Mike Featherstone & Scott Lash (eds.) *Spaces of Culture: City, Nation, World* (London: Sage, 1999), pp. 49–63. p. 62. This echoes Alonso and Oiarzabal's view that, "[on] the Internet, all of us are "immigrants" who simultaneously share a common space called cyberspace." Alonso & Oiarzaba, Diasporas in a New Media Age, p.11.
[72] Roland Robertson 'Glocalization: Time-Space and Homogeneity-Heterogeneity'. In Mike Featherstone, Scott Lash and Roland Robertson (eds.) Global Modernities (London: Sage, 1995), pp. 25-44.
[73] John A. Guidry, Michael D. Kennedy & Mayer N. Zald (eds.), Globalizations and Social Movements: Culture, Power, and the Transnational Public Sphere (Ann Arbor: University of Michigan Press, 2001). p. 12.

[74] Nir Rosen "Ghosts in the mosques", *Al-Jazeera*, (30 September 2011) http://www.aljazeera.com/indepth/features/2011/09/201193063322274258.html [accessed 2 October].

[75] "Kurdish activist among latest killed in Syria", *Al-Jazeera* (8 October 2011) http://www.aljazeera.com/news/middleeast/2011/10/2011107172252384438.html [accessed 31 October 2011].

[76] Nir Rosen "Syria's symphony of scorn", *Al-Jazeera*, (30 September 2011) http://www.aljazeera.com/indepth/features/2011/09/2011930102056270682.html [accessed 2 October].

[77] Lauren Williams, "Syria's prankster army make case for non-violence" *The Daily Star* (31 October 2011) http://www.dailystar.com.lb/News/Middle-East/2011/Oct-31/152623-syrias-prankster-army-make-case-for-non-violence.ashx#ixzz1cRRAXixj [accessed 1 November 2011].

[78] "President al-Assad Delivers Speech at People's Assembly", *Syrian Arab News Agency* (30th March 2011) http://www.sana.sy/eng/21/2011/03/30/pr-339334.htm [accessed 12 October 2011].

[79] http://trash.vsyria.com [accessed 15 October 2011]. Website appears to have been removed by November 2012.

[80] "Speech of H.E. President Bashar al-Assad at Damascus University on the situation in Syria", *Syrian Arab News Agency* (21 June 2011) http://www.sana.sy/eng/337/2011/06/21/353686.htm [accessed 10 October 2011].

[81] Helmi Noman, "The Emergence of Open and Organized Pro-Government Cyber Attacks in the Middle East: The Case of the Syrian Electronic Army", *Information Warfare Monitor* (May 30, 2011).

[82] "Speech of H.E. President Bashar al-Assad at Damascus University on the situation in Syria", *Syrian Arab News Agency* (21 June 2011) http://www.sana.sy/eng/337/2011/06/21/353686.htm [accessed 10 October 2011]. Asad's exact words were "The army consists of the brothers of every Syrian citizen...*There is the electronic army which has been a real army in virtual reality*."

[83] Helmi Noman, "The Emergence of Open and Organized Pro-Government Cyber Attacks in the Middle East".

[84] Ironically, oppositional cyberactivists have used the same software to target Syrian government and pro-regime websites such as Organization of Radio and TV, Addounia TV, and news websites syriarose.com and syria-news.com.

[85] Fiddaalidin Al-Sayed Issa, author's interview. (11 May 2011).

[86] Amnesty International Report, "The Long Reach of the Mukhabaraat: Violence and Harassment Against Syrians Abroad and Their Relatives Back Home" (London: Amnesty International Publications, 2011). p.8.

[87] Christophe Ayad, Beatings in Paris Show how far Syrian Regime will Go to Pursue Dissenters, *Le Monde/Worldcrunch*, (October 7, 2011) http://www.worldcrunch.com/beatings-paris-show-how-far-syrian-regime-will-go-pursue-dissenters/3894 [accessed October 11, 2011].

[88] *Amnesty International Report*," The Long Reach of the Mukhabaraat". pp. 9-10.

[89] Del Quentin Wilber, "Mohamad Soueid of N.Va. accused of surveilling anti-Assad protests for Syrian officials", *Washington Post*, (13 October 2011) http://www.washingtonpost.com/local/mohamad-soueid-of-nva-accused-of-spying-for-syrian-officials/2011/10/12/gIQAPWEIgL_story.html [accessed 20 October 2011].

[90] Elie Chalala , "Light vs. Darkness: How the Syrian Opposition & Assad Regime Approach the Media", *Al-Jadid*, (2011) Vol. 16, no. 62. p.1.

[91] "Syrians living abroad say it is too late to accept any reforms from Assad", *Al-Arabiya*, (03 October 2011) http://www.alarabiya.net/articles/2011/10/03/169941.html [accessed 5 October 2011].

[92] Anthony Shadid, "Key Syrian City Takes On the Tone of a Civil War", *New York Times* (October 1, 2011) http://www.nytimes.com/2011/10/02/world/middleeast/homs-syria-spirals-down-toward-civil-war.html?pagewanted=all [accessed October 11, 2011].

[93] Jasmine Roman, "Damascus's upper class clings to its privileged illusions", *The National*, (7 November 2011) http://www.thenational.ae/thenationalconversation/comment/damascuss-upper-class-clings-to-its-privileged-illusions [accessed 8 November].

[94] Jon W. Anderson, "Mediatized Islam, Cyberspace and the Public Sphere", Prepared for Conference on "The Challenges of Integrating Islam: Comparative Experiences of Europe and the Middle East", Institute for Middle East Studies, George Washington University (February 14, 2008). Available at http://faculty.cua.edu/anderson/mediatised%20islam3.pdf.

[95] Guidry, Kennedy & Zald, *"Globalizations and Social Movements"*. p. 11.

[96] Anderson, *"Imagined Communities"*.

3
Celebrity Politics in Troubled Times: The Case of Muna Wassef[1]
Helena Nassif

Introduction

Visiting Damascus in June 2011 three months into the start of the domestic unrest, I was at a friend's place when asked whether I knew about a women-only protest that had taken place in the streets of Al-Midan, a Damascene neighbourhood, with protestors chanting "Umm Joseph... Umm Joseph."[2] Out of all the television characters played by Muna Wassef, one of the most famous contemporary Syrian actresses, the interest of this case study focuses on her role in the popular television series Bab el-Hara (The Neighbourhood Gate) seasons four and five as Umm Joseph.[3] The study juxtaposes this fictional role with her real life experience during the first months of the uprising. The fictitious heroic character Umm Joseph has been the subject of multiple controversies and has been criticized for not being "real," by both critics and the public.[4] The character is best revealed in a short description of the closing scene of Bab el-Hara season five. The camera pans on all the neighbourhood men standing in a semi-circle addressing moral messages to a traitor before his public execution. To the side of the majority male crowd, Umm Joseph with her face visible and a cross to her chest stands with a group of women with their faces covered. Before the men start shooting, Umm Joseph hands her gun to the spy's wife who publicly asks for divorce and shoots the first bullet in revenge. The scene ends with Umm Joseph shouting "Oh people, a country whose women's and men's hands are clutched together, will have its head held up high with no one able to reach it." The significance of studying the case of Muna Wassef and discussing the character of Umm Joseph stems from the fact that the women who took to the streets of al-Midan neighbourhood in Damascus in 2011 were specifically chanting the name of a fictitious character "Umm Joseph." The drama text in this case provides the entry point to study the political.

The beginning of the Syrian protests in March 2011 led to a division in the country between regime loyalists and the opposition. This division was reflected in the position of popular television stars whose public image became vulnerable to accusations of treason. Wassef, together with more than one hundred workers in the television drama industry, signed a Call asking the Syrian troops to allow goods to reach "besieged" children in a Syrian border town. The call was evaluated as "anti-patriotic," and many production houses threatened to boycott the signatories. In the case of Wassef, who was accused of treason, I look at how tensions over public expressions of loyalty reflect the conflict over defining and claiming the state.

The description which follows narrates the events that took place after the release of the Call during May 2011 so as to, first, investigate the context that led Wassef's fictional role to impose "the promise" of the hero over her everyday life and, second, to document the connections between celebrities and processes of negotiating patriotism during the beginning of the conflict (May-July 2011).[5] This case study focuses on how the accusation of treason against one star actress can provide initial insight into the complex public struggle over of the Syrian state during the uprising.

Television Stars, Humanitarian Calls and the Politics of Loyalty

At the end of April 2011, more than one month into the protests, a petition dubbed the "Urgent Call to the Syrian Government for the Children of Daraa" (or the "Call for Milk" as named by the pro-regime loyalists) was signed by Muna Wassef along with more than 100 artists, media personalities and scriptwriters. The petition asked the Syrian government to allow the passage of milk to children in the "besieged" southern city Daraa.[6] Loyalists saw the Call as "anti-regime" propaganda, as it wrongly accused the army of blockading the city, while "pro-demonstration" intellectuals were unhappy with its language evaluating it as apolitical, not courageous enough and not calling the problem by its name.[7] Despite the "humane" language of the one-paragraph Call, loyalists accused it of crossing the line that safeguards the image of the national army as the protector of the people. Rima Fleihan, scriptwriter and the author of the call, came under a great deal of pressure as a result of her initiative, and saw her reputation smeared, which led her to retract the Call under the pretext that the signatories did not have enough information about the situation of children in Daraa.

The "Call" triggered a number of debates on various media outlets including public and private television channels that hosted loyalist actors who publicly supported the government stance. The shows invited artists to condemn their "disloyal" colleagues for taking the "pro-demonstrators" position. In Arabic, an accusation of treason has a specific word, *at-takhween*. *At-takhween* is not a legal accusation *per se*, as much as a discursive one that aims to delegitimize the political position of the accused. At the same time, *at-takhween* is a pejorative word that is used against the process itself, making the accusation seem trivial. Intellectuals and journalists criticized the *at-takhween* process and attacked what they called a culture of *takhween* (accusation of treason).

Early in May 2011, one program on Syrian public television hosted Muna Wassef along with two female actresses Yara Sabri and Kinda Alloush, one male actor/director Maher Slaibi and one female director Rasha Sharbatji who had all signed the Call.[8] Wassef stated that she was not mistaken but misunderstood and apologized if she had been misunderstood. She specified that she was defending her patriotism and not herself as an individual or citizen. She was wearing the Syrian flag on the left lapel of her black jacket and talking with enthusiasm. Following her equivocal justification, the host asked accusingly whether signatories had intended to abuse their position as stars or the people's appreciation of their art and continued, "the Call was translated into four languages, too bad it was translated into four languages, even the Israeli media has discussed this Call and maybe it was taken as a document by other channels and human rights organizations, how can we reply to this?"[9]

The anchor's use of the word Israel was enough to put the artists on the defensive. His role provides an example of what Wedeen (1999) regards as "disciplinary-symbolic power" where lines of demarcation between ruler and ruled are complex and shifting since the anchor, once ruled, is in the studio context playing the ruler (p.150). His interrogating style led the stars participating in the program to dissociate themselves from any misuse of the Call by foreign powers. The anchor was repeating similar accusations found in various articles online or in posts and groups on Facebook accusing the artists of treason.

On the 14th of May, approximately two weeks after the Call was published, president al-Asad met with a number of celebrity artists. According to Wassef, he rejected all accusations of treason and stressed that each of the artists' actions was rooted in their patriotic loyalty.[10] Wassef appreciated the president's consideration for artists, but still thought that his intervention came after harm had already been done.

She was deeply hurt by the accusations that had come after a fifty-year career filled with flattery, part of which was from the ruling regime and its institutions. For instance, in 2009 she received the Syrian Order of Merit-Excellent from President Bashar al-Asad, acclaiming her role in serving her country through Syrian and Arab Television and Cinema. The press celebrated Wassef when she was honoured by the ruling party's youth association in March 2010.[11]

Meeting with the president did not put an end to *at-takhween* practices. On the 22nd of May 2011, the private pro-regime channel Al-Dunia, hosted actors Bassem Yakhuor, Abbas al-Nouri, Amal Arafa, Fahd el-Abed and director Seif Eddine Sibai who did not sign the Call, and did not contradict the regime's discourse but tried to avoid accusing their colleagues of treason. The anchor contacted Rima Fleihan by phone to talk to fellow artists in the studio and she was accusingly asked to explain why she had taken the decision to write the Call. She read a press release where she confirmed that she was not ready to work with any "foreign entity," she apologized for what might have been misunderstood and emphasized that she had written the Call with, "the best of intentions in a moment of high emotion" driven by a "sense of motherhood, without thinking that the Call would have been abused, distorted and exaggerated."[12]

"Accusing the Artists of Treason: The Series is on and with Great Success," was the title of one article in the press in Lebanon following the airing of the public television chat show.[13] The Syrian writer criticized the accusation process (*at-takhween*) that had divided the artists into traitors and patriots. He scrutinized the new standards of patriotism and asked whether the famous television drama series director Najdat Anzour was setting these standards. Anzour had initiated a statement during early May 2011, signed by Syrian production houses, to boycott the artists who had signed the "Urgent Call to the Syrian Government for the Children of Daraa". The campaign's statement was signed by twenty-two production houses including 'Aaj Production, the producer of the first two seasons of Bab el-Hara. The declaration accused the "Call" to have been based on the "fabricated claims of unknown witnesses and activists in suspicious foreign circles." It added that the signatories should have contacted the Ministries of Economy and Health to check on the food supplies available in Daraa before signing a Call written in the "US Facebook circles known for their blatant hostility to our country and all it represents." Israel was also mentioned in the statement that "draws the attention" of the signatories to the fact that the bullets fired at the army are "Israeli bullets par excellence."[14]

Director and producer Haitham Haqqi, one of the main founders of the Syrian television drama industry, was keen to be amongst those who took a strong stance against Anzour's statement. He denounced it in an article published under the title "Those Alien Attitudes" where he refused all accusations or threats against artists' livelihood.[15] Haqqi's article was one among a number of other articles in the Syrian online press, which reported on the production houses' statement and on the alleged demand that Muna Wassef be stripped of the Syrian Order of Merit that she had been awarded by President al-Asad in 2009. The sentence asking to strip Wassef of the medal was however missing from the published text signed by the production houses. It is difficult to assess whether the sentence had been originally included in the written statement, or simply was rumoured to be so.

In an alleged interview, Anzour stated that the production houses had intended to teach the artists who had signed the Call "a lesson."[16] He added that they would not boycott the artists after the latter apologized, "they are our friends and it is not personal." Thus, Anzour drew a line between the public and private and by defining the issue as public he requested the popular artists to take a clear position. Similarly to the anchor in the context of the studio, he was playing the role of the ruler trying to enforce compliance upon artists. The case of Muna Wassef provides an example of how the public expression of a star was believed to be politically significant, leading to its containment.

Muna Wassef the Star

Muna Wassef (1942), a self-made professional actress who is recognised to have succeeded as a result of her talent and achievement might be the most acclaimed female star in Syria with a fan base that extends across the Arab world. Her filmography includes Moustapha Akkad's classic 'The Message'.[17] She began her career as a model when she was seventeen years old, then joined the Military Institution Theatre when she was eighteen. She got married to the Syrian film director Muhammad Shahin, who died in 2003, and gave birth to one child Ammar, who is one of the dissident voices in exile.

Syrian novelist and scriptwriter, Khaled Khalifeh, divided the artists into those indebted to the regime for their fame and those self-made.[18] For the former, he used the term "consecrated" in Arabic to explain how certain artists became successful irrespective of their talents. The regime, he continued, expected loyalty from all artists. The links between the owners of the production houses and the political establishment are difficult to map but not impossible to establish. Out of the eleven main businessmen whom the opposition accuses of benefiting from and serving the status quo, three are well known to have had a hand in the development of the drama industry. The son of Abdul Halim Khaddam, ex-vice president who defected from the regime in 2005, owned el-Cham International for Cinema and Television Production. The company was one of the first private production houses of the nineties, closed after the family escaped to Paris. Mohammad Hamsho owns Syria International for Art Production, a major production house in the country, and Majd Suleiman, the son of a former high- ranking army commander, owns United Group that organizes a yearly Oscar-like prize "Adonia" which holds tributes to the Syrian Drama and the efforts of its creative personnel (2004-2010).

Rojek (2001) differentiates between three forms of celebrity status; the "ascribed" (lineage-dependent), "achieved" (accomplishment-dependent) and "attributed" (media representation dependent) which he calls "celetoids" (p. 18-19). In his analysis he does not give special attention to the role of the state in creating media hype. In contrast, Khalifeh does not highlight the role of the media, but that of the state, in attributing the consecrated celebrity.[19] In the context of Syria, it is important to mention that the status achieved/attributed is not only dependent on the perceived accomplishments or media exposure of the star but his/her relation with the security apparatus and the rewards gained as a result of this relation. "Muna Wassef comes from another time," Khalifeh insists. Her fame, he explains, has been achieved "before the rise of the Gulf funded Syrian drama" of the last two decades, which allowed for the development of the "attributed" celebrity status. Khalifeh mentions Wassef's "memorable roles," her dedication to acting and her knowledge of the craft before it became a good business. All of these can explain why she was able to resist offering her "full loyalty," according to Khalifeh.[20]

When talking about her attitude towards the on-going events Wassef did not clearly mention whether she was anti or pro-regime, but specified that she was pro-reform:[21]

> Irrespective of the problem I faced, the country remains the most important thing. When I played the part of Umm Joseph I believed in something, not only Umm Joseph but all my roles during the last fifty years, that for me, Syria is a red line. This is my country and whatever happens, I am not ready to leave, you know, God forbid if anything happens, I won't leave, this is my conviction exactly like that of Umm Joseph, she has something that resembles me. If other people leave, I stay with insistence. I mean I can't love the country when it's strong and leave it when it's wounded. ... During the last few years, when I

played the character of a strong woman, it was because I wanted to feel stronger internally, because they used to challenge me 'what would the beautiful coquette achieve'! And then I proved to be successful. I chose roles that made me stronger, my general knowledge and my theatre experience all helped make me who I am. ... I am with reform and with what has happened [meaning the protests] but without reaching the stage of wounding the country. So no human is killed, so I don't witness blood either from the protesters or from the army or police, so we do not reach the phase we are in. I mean I am falling in love with Syria more and more. I have seen a lot, I am not young, I have seen those who have been displaced when they left their countries, I have seen when the Americans entered Iraq, where is Iraq now? In the end this is not the way problems are solved, this is what I believe in. In a way, it resembles my roles but when they ask where is Umm Joseph they are asking me to be more, they are asking me to be Umm Joseph the one on the screen, but it is too much, and I am not, not, not Umm Joseph.

During the whole interview, Wassef celebrated an idealised representation of homeland and disregarded the view of Syria as equivalent to the president. She considered Syria itself to be a "red line" - its problems being more important than her own. She stressed that whatever happens, she would not leave and compared herself to Umm Joseph who had "something that resembles her ... the attachment to the house that harbours the photos of members of the family who are gone."

Wedeen (1999) mentions an incident when Wassef, "Syria's most famous actress, declared to her television audience that it was raining – a welcome occurrence in desert regions – because Syrians were holding a referendum reaffirming their loyalty and allegiance to Hafiz al-Asad." (p.39). Capitalising on her past declared loyalty to the regime, Wassef mentions, during the only television interview she gave after signing the Call, her volunteer role during the 1973 war and how artists were invited by late president Hafez al-Asad and thanked for being "soldiers inside the country and not on the border."[22] Although Wassef surely fulfils the criteria of an "achieved" celebrity, in a sense she could not escape being part of what Khalifeh criticizes; the regime's role in "consecrating" television stars into "national symbols."[23] Her past expressions of loyalty to the regime, even if or when discrepant from privately held belief, complexifies the use of these set statuses. The blurring of these forms of celebrity statuses and their inability to provide a meaningful explanation of Wassef's political positionality requires a different type of investigation that examines how the meanings of state, regime and country interfere in how Wassef and other stars situate or are situated as "insiders" or "traitors" within the public sphere.

Implicating Fiction in Protest

Talking about Umm Joseph, Wassef, who is born to a Syrian Christian mother and a Syrian Kurdish Muslim father, explains:

> The designer and I were able to develop her distinct looks. She shouldn't resemble any of the neighbourhood women ... She should look Christian and I added the human touch based on the modes of speech used by Christian women like referring to Jesus and the Virgin Mary that they use and I use since my mother's upbringing has affected me ... Umm Joseph resembles the woman I want [to be] in life, I mean I am not the subservient type to start with and neither was my mother ... I loved (Umm Joseph) because she was courageous and because she was noble. I loved her because the reality of the situation in Syria is that all sects are together. I have not seen, in my long life, conflict between Christians and Muslims. I witness this coexistence and believe in its message that this character wants to deliver.

When I asked Muna Wassef about the anti-regime women-only protest in Al-Midan, chanting "Umm Joseph," she smiled and asked her sister who was sitting with us whether she knew about it. She then asked me whether I had seen the Al-Jazeera report comparing her life stances to those of her fictional role.[24] The audience "wanted to make me a heroine!" she added. As if the protestors used "Umm Joseph" as a borrowed element from one story used to tell another story. Umm Joseph is not an ordinary character, but that of a strong independent woman who participates together with men in armed struggle against the French army. Informants in Damascus explained that the Christian name (Umm Joseph) was raised in a predominantly Muslim neighbourhood (al-Midan) as a means to call Syrian Christians to join the protests or to highlight the unity of Syrians across sectarian divides. There are other possible explanations; however here I would argue that by chanting "Umm Joseph," it is as if the protestors had liberated a fragment from the dominant discourse and infused it into everyday life. In other words, they released the fictional character from its discursive ensemble thus confronting the power of the screen and reclaiming the power to recount the narrative. Umm Joseph, and not Muna Wassef, was called for in the protest. The women chanting were celebrating the actress' role as if aiming to repossess lifeworld stories packaged as discourse (De Certeau 1984). To call out to Umm Joseph at that moment in time was to redefine the "patriotic."

The weaving of the personal as political with the fictitious is also evident in the way the director of Bab el-Hara season five, Mo'men Malla, worked with Wassef. He allowed her to improvise lines into the dialogue for example in one scene Umm Joseph with her eyes swollen with tears whispered: "the strange land (*el-ghorbeh*) has eaten my children." In the interview, Wassef added, "my son is also living in exile (*ghorbeh*)." The interpolation of Wassef's lived emotions and experience into her fictional character and the affective meaning attached to the Arabic word "*ghorbeh*" (translated to strange land or expatriation) might help explain the power of her utterance in the fictional role. But, what if this "lost" child is accused of treason? Muna Wassef is not the mother of Joseph but the mother of Ammar whose loyalty is made suspect.

Ammar Abdulhamid

Wassef is a special case among Syrian actresses and actors who are not fully supportive of the regime since her son is living in, and accused of being funded by, the United States of America. The son Ammar Abdulhamid (1966) introduces himself on his blog entitled "Syrian Revolution Digest" as a "liberal democracy activist whose anti-regime activities led to his exile from Syria on September 7, 2005." He is the founder and director of the Tharwa Foundation, "a non-profit dedicated to democracy promotion."[25] Abdulhamid is an ex-fellow at the Saban Center and a current fellow at the Foundation for Defense of Democracies (FDD) both regarded to be pro-Israeli. When asked why he was allowed to leave the country and not jailed like other dissidents, he suspected that it was due to his mother Muna Wassef.[26]

A published New York Times "encounter" with Abdulhamid confirms the three main accusations pro-regime activists use to attack Muna Wassef on various online forums. Wassef's son is first, open to working with Israelis. Second, he has relations with the US government and had met "leading figures in the Bush administration" and third, he admires the US position and was "hoping to spend the next year explaining the American viewpoint to anyone in Damascus who would listen."[27] Tharwa's two pages on Facebook have a total of 122 members or people who "like" it while his personal public figure page on Facebook has 215 people who like it.[28] In the same magazine article, Jon Alterman from the Center for Strategic and International Studies in Washington considers liberals like Abdulhamid to be "too westernized to make an impact on the Arab masses." With the changes in the region, Abdulhamid's role is difficult to evaluate at the moment. He has contributed testimony to the Senate foreign relations committee.[29] Joshua Landis, author of "Syria Comment" newsletter and head of the Center for Middle East Studies at the University of Oklahoma, wrote on

29 March 2011 that Abdulhamid has "emerged as the 'unofficial spokesman' and most visible face of the Syrian Revolutionary movement" in the US.[30] Irrespective of Abdulhamid's actual influence on the dissident street or his impact on US foreign policy in regard to the Syrian government, his political activity puts him in a questionable position and makes his mother vulnerable to accusations.

The Syrian regime's rhetoric positions the Syrian state in confrontation with the United States and Israel, a political line dubbed "*mumana'a*" in Arabic which translates as "rejectionism," "anti-conspiracy" or "anti-imperialism" in contrast to the other camp of pro-Western "moderates" such as Mubarak's Egypt. This rhetoric emphasizes the neo-imperial US policies and disrespect of international law for example in regard to the occupation of Iraq, supporting Israel and interfering in Syria's internal affairs. This same rhetoric potentially puts the state's subjects in a polarized position of "patriots" versus "traitors." It is beyond the scope of this paper to further analyse how the US "War on Terror," Manichean policies and attitudes compare to the black and white representations the Syrian government uses vis-à-vis the US. However, emphasizing the dominance of such a discourse, which is interrelated with US foreign policies, might explain how allies or defenders of the US, like Abdulhamid, are made suspect. Wassef stressed that her son is against external military intervention in Syria.[31] In this case, she is speaking from within the discourse that renders those supportive of military intervention as "servants to the imperial hegemony." Her son's position during June 2011 allowed her to open a window within the local dominant rhetoric to argue that, "Abdulhamid is patriotic in his own way." Her attempt at defending her son's patriotism became more problematic after he called for military intervention in an interview with the Israeli newspaper Yedioth Ahronoth in December 2011 entitled the "World should Bomb Syria" thus rendering him her weak spot.[32]

Mother and Son: "Public" or "Private"

The treason accusation campaign targeted the personal link portraying Wassef as responsible for her son's politics as if disowning him would prove her loyalty to the country or regime. Wassef refused to choose between her son and her country. She stressed the fact that she is an independent entity with her own opinions and stances which she is able to take and defend without the influence of patriarchy, a son or a husband. Secondly, she refused to either defend or attack her son's politics and put her relation with him outside her public life, back into the private. "He has his way of loving the country and I have my reasons to be annoyed why they spoke."[33] While she did not specify who "they" were or "why" they spoke, she made it clear that the de-legitimization discourse targeted her public persona through her (private) blood ties to a dissident expatriate. Wassef became the victim of a triple-edged struggle for power, 1) an internal one with a dominant national discourse that defines patriotism as antagonistic to empire, 2) the U.S. and its interests in the region and 3) gender politics reflected in her position as a woman and a mother.

Wassef the star has clear ideas about her career, roles and aspirations. She does not perceive herself as merely a wife or a mother. However, the view of women as wives or mothers persists and the accusations targeting Wassef cast her as a mother, either responsible for her son's deeds, or under the authority of his political position. Wassef refused to be described as an annex to her son and emphasized her independence. She regarded motherhood to be a private business. Fleihan (the scriptwriter, author of the Call), on the other hand, used motherhood as an excuse to deemphasise an "irrational" act that stemmed from her emotional attachment to the children of Daraa. Fleihan was presumably forced to depoliticize her position, while on the other hand Wassef politicized her silence by choosing to stay away from the media after her television appearance.

Wassef and Fleihan's presence in the public domain forced them to tactically use notions of the "private' and "public" to negotiate accusations of treason. While Wassef's interest was to draw a strict border between the "private" and the "public", Fleihan saw value in extending the "private" to the "public." In the slightly different context of reality television shows viewed in Kuwait and Lebanon, Kraidy (2010) asks the relevant question of "why did women emerge as powerful and contested symbols?" (p.196). He concludes that in times of war women stars are vulnerable to "symbolic appropriation" especially when the nation is fragile and "feelings of belonging to imagined national communities" are heightened (p. 196). Times of conflict allow for "instances of women's victimization as symbolic pawns of nations or as repositories of traditions;" meanwhile women are politically engaged, participating in demonstrations and in some cases confronting "self-appointed custodians of tradition" (p. 197). This case study provides additional evidence of the centrality of gender in the study of power. Further analysis on how the accusation of treason is not only a means to discipline dissent but a mediated reflection of the problematic of nationhood, is part of my ongoing research on the construction and tension between regime, state and homeland discourses and loyalties.

Patriotism in Question

One characteristic of stars, which they share with power elites, is their search for privacy in isolation from other groups in society (Alberoni 1972, p.70). This "absence of mutuality" with audiences, who know the stars without the stars knowing them, leads to the construction of a star image. During the first part of the interview, Wassef described her deliberate choice of roles of strong women. As was stated above, she chose these roles because she needed to become strong herself, the roles reflected strength back on her. Later she infused her strength into the roles of weak women. While Wassef personified strength and power in roles where she confronted patriarchy and colonialism like that of Umm Joseph, she fell short of maintaining her established star image as the hero when she stressed in the interview that she was not what the protestors expected.

The role of a hero in the non-fiction world, which Wassef did not play, was instead assumed by a young actress Fadwa Suleiman, who moved to Homs and lived in a rebellious neighbourhood leading demonstrations together with a local star football player.[34] The case study of Suleiman and other actresses such as May Skaff are beyond the scope of this paper; however, they provide important material for further analysis and future research that aims to discuss the varied roles of stars during the Syrian uprising. The case of Wassef shows how a star who participated in supporting the demonstrations, by signing a Call that questioned whether children were infiltrators, did not enjoy the chance to have her charisma employed within the struggle to confront the state's discourse on patriotism. Wassef's charisma was managed through an accusation of treason campaign, which further led most stars to withdraw from the public debate. The majority of stars succumbed to being marginalised from the political scene unless they were regime supporters.

Loyalists (TV presenters, television drama directors, cyberactivists, etc.) used the accusation of treason as a way to manage the position of stars who were attempting to employ their charisma to question or deconstruct the regime's label of who is a patriot and who is a traitor. The regime's grip over the definition of patriotism allowed loyalists to mobilize in this way. It is difficult to fully explain the various factors influencing the positions of stars accepting their public role to be constrained, including Wassef, nevertheless it is important to highlight a few comments. First, it is difficult to know without further research whether loyalty or compliance with the regime remains a result of its power or other factors including ideology and fear of insecurity resulting from the threat of Lebanonization in Syria. Second, the division in the country between loyalists and opposition had not polarized the whole population and a large section of society remained silent, i.e. not publicly aligning with any side. Alberoni (1972) stresses that the status of stars is always "potentially revocable: by the public" (p.74). This complicates the argument, because artists might have been influenced by a desire to safeguard relations with audiences. Dissidents, on the other hand tried to redefine treason by raising the slogan: "a traitor is the one who kills his people," something Hajj Saleh (2012) regards as a revolutionary definition that constitutes the basis for a new patriotism.[35] Among the silent majority are stars who express worry at accusations by dissidents suspecting stars still residing in Syria to be regime loyalists.[36] Amidst this instability challenging the regime and negotiating the Syrian state and nation, the symbolic power of a star like Muna Wassef did not translate into political power to participate in redefining the patriotic and contributing to political consensus.

Conclusion

Going back to the women's protest chanting the name of a television character from a fictional story, the protestors in Damascus participated in the battle to define the patriotic by choosing to shout Umm Joseph. Umm Joseph as a symbol represented the action of Muna Wassef signing the Call and the narrative of Umm Joseph fighting the French. The use of this symbol by the protestors was a creative use of the institutional narrative against itself. Umm Joseph, the patriot according to the regime's narrative, is also Wassef, the patriot according to protestors. Umm Joseph became the complex symbol contesting the official patriotism with the aim of redefining it. The official patriotic discourse claims to stand firm against foreign neo-imperial forces and advocates Asad's personalization of power. Umm Joseph on the other hand defies the mandate, which is the historical counterpart of today's neo-imperialism. She does that out of loyalty to Syria, the land, the imagined community, not the president.

This paper is an attempt at demonstrating how conflicting accounts of patriotisms struggled in a mediated sphere of multiple players. Producers, famous directors, scriptwriters, journalists, actors and actresses acted through various media in order to make their cases heard. The national private and public television, pan Arab satellite television, Lebanese press, Facebook, websites and blogs were all spaces for blaming and defending, defaming and honouring. In this process Muna Wassef, by signing the Call, made herself liable to become a contested site in the battle for power. By fighting patriarchy and colonialism in her fictional roles, Wassef was asked by the public and forbidden by the power elites to play a role that would generalize her charisma. While she took a political position to withdraw from the public sphere after the televised appearance following the Call, one group of women protesting used her fictional role as a symbol to fight the Syrian regime's definition of patriotism. To question the workings of treason and loyalty in the case of Muna Wassef is part of a continuous project that sheds light on the challenges of mediatised practices in a decolonial state living through conflict and transition that is threatening its existence.

---

[1] The author would like to thank Muna Wassef, Khaled Khalifa and the anonymous interlocutors for their generous and genuine exchange at a time that was filled with the insecurity of transition. She would also like to thank Lisa Wedeen, Nikolas Kosmatopoulos, Sami Hermes, Layal Ftouni and Tarik Sabry for their constructive comments during the phase when the intellectual endeavour seemed futile in the face of human suffering.

[2] Umm Joseph, Arabic for "mother of Joseph", is the name of the character played by Muna Wassef in Bab el-Hara (see footnote 3).

[3] Bab el-Hara (subject of PhD research) is a hit Ramadan drama series of five seasons (thirty episodes-) aired on MBC, the Saudi pan Arab channel. Bab el-Hara tells the story of the life-world of a fictitious Damascene neighbourhood under the French mandate during the first half of the 20th century. Season five (2010) narrates how the life of this neighbourhood was unsettled due to its infiltration by a Syrian collaborator working for the French army.

[4] The character has been criticized as to the number of French soldiers she killed while engaging with the national resistance against the French mandate army and the unlikeliness that only one Christian woman be part of the lifeworld of a Muslim neighbourhood.

[5] Looking into research on stardom, celebrity, and fame, I have come across few researches that drift away from representational text-based or discursive individual-based studies. Turner (2010) identifies four angles to approach the study of celebrities; 1) as a genre of representation, 2) as a discursive effect on those 'celebritised', 3) as an industry and 4) as a cultural formation that has a social function. Turner criticizes the second trend for framing the "representational regime" or the "process of celebritisation" in terms of an "individual seeking validation of ... their intrinsic 'star' quality" and argues that the production/mediating process is of higher influence than "the recognition of the particular qualities of each individual self" (p. 14). He highlights that most of the literature on stars falls within the first two trends and calls for research to adopt a social or political economy approach that situates the celebrity within the socio-economic issues and dilemmas she/he engages.

[6] "We the undersigned demand that the Syrian Government stop its five-day-old blockade on Daraa and its villages. The blockade has led to a shortage in food and other essential supplies necessary for subsistence which has affected innocent children who could not be 'infiltrators' (*mundasseen*) in any of the gangs or the different sedition (*fetna*) projects. Based on the above,

we demand that food and medicine supplies and children's food be permitted to Daraa under the supervision of the Syrian Ministry of Health and the Red Crescent. We do not want the children of our country to be hungry or hurt. We hope for immediate action." Translated from Arabic by the author.

[7] Author's interviews.
[8] http://www.youtube.com/watch?v=Jn3J6EJZ4TA&feature=related.
[9] Ibid.
[10] Author's interview.
[11] http://www.discover-syria.com/news/5975.
[12] Translated from Arabic by the author. http://www.youtube.com/watch?v=GvaPPTe17oY&feature=related.
[13] Suleiman, Hazem (2011) Accusing the Artists of Treason: The Series is on and with Great Success. Al-Akhbar Newspaper. Issue 1406 Monday 9 May. http://www.al-akhbar.com/node/11661.
[14] See article: Unknown (2011) Production Companies: We Refute the Latest Call by the Intellectuals and the Artists Regarding Daraa and We Declare our Boycott of those Who Signed it. Syria News. http://www.syria-news.com/var/articlem.php?id=14956.
[15] See article: Haqqi, Haitham (2011) Those Alien Attitudes. Syria-News. http://www.syria-news.com/readnews.php?sy_seq=132638.
[16] See article: Nweisati, Rola (2011) Najdat Anzour: Some Artists Signed the 'Call for Milk' as a result of Stupidity or Ignorance. Syria Days. http://www.syriadays.com/index.php?mode=article&id=5903.
[17] For more information visit The Message page on the Internet Movie Database http://www.imdb.com/title/tt0074896/.
[18] Author's interview.
[19] Author's interview.
[20] Author's interview.
[21] Author's interview.
[22] http://www.youtube.com/watch?v=Jn3J6EJZ4TA&feature=related
[23] Author's interview.
[24] Al Jazeera broadcasted a five-minute report on the 15th of May 2011 that opened with images from the protests in Syria edited into images from Bab el-Hara. The journalist commented:

> The inhabitants of Al Dabe' neighbourhood [the neighbourhood's fictitious name in the series] are no longer united, their renowned long drama series of five seasons has long ended and they have found themselves facing a real struggle in their country, one that requests them to take a clear position independent of art. Is this the sixth season of Bab El-Hara, that the Arab audience is watching now, where the Syrian Drama stars or most of them have been forced to take off their acting clothes and disclose their principles, their fears or maybe their interests and personal benefits? The answer reveals that the moment which divided the actors, was when the Syrian Army tanks entered the city of Daraa.

Translated from Arabic by the author. http://www.youtube.com/watch?v=O8FlL123osM.

[25] Ammar Abdulhamid (2012) About the Author. Syrian Revolution Digest. http://www.syrianrevolutiondigest.com/.

[26] Smith, Lee (2005) A Liberal in Damascus. The New York Times Magazine. http://www.nytimes.com/2005/02/13/magazine/13ENCOUNTER.html.

[27] Ibid.

[28] Accessed during August 2011. Accessing the pages during February 2012, Thawra's two facebook pages have a total of 136 likes while Abdulhamid's public figure page reached 416 likes and his personal facebook profile 1018 subscribers.

[29] The contribution took place on the 9th of November 2011 to the subcommittee on near Eastern and south central Asian affairs and the written report was titled 'Towards a Post-Assad Syria: Options for the United States and Like-Minded Nations to Further Assist the Anti-Regime Syrian Opposition.' Available from http://www.defenddemocracy.org/testimony/us-policy-in-syria.

[30] Landis, Joshua (2001) Ammar Abdulhamid Emerges as Face of the Syrian Revolution, According to Washington Times. Syria Comment. http://www.joshualandis.com/blog/?p=8864&cp=all#comments.

[31] Author's interview in June 2011.

[32] Azoulay, Orly (2011) World Should Bomb Syria. Yedioth Internet. http://www.ynetnews.com/articles/0,7340,L-4168102,00.html. The sub heading of the article reads "Special: In first interview with Israeli media, two Syrian exiles urge world to wake up." This interview was not the first Abdulhamid had given to the Israeli press. For more information see Benhorin, Yitzhak (2007) Towards a Democratic Syria. Yedioth Internet. http://www.ynetnews.com/articles/0,7340,L-3369003,00.html.

[33] Author's interview.

[34] For more information see Oweis, Khaled Yacoub (2012) Syrian Actress Treads New Stage in Syrian Protests. Reuters. http://www.reuters.com/article/2012/01/05/us-syria-actress-idUSTRE8040WQ20120105.

[35] Hajj Saleh, Yassine (2012) The Party is no Longer the Leader of the State and Society. Al Hayat.

[36] Author's interview.

Appendix
Memorandum of the Advisory Committee about the Internal Situation on the Verge of the Second Decade of the Leadership of your Excellency[1]

Mr President,

Introduction:

By the summer of 2010 Syria will have completed its first decade under the leadership of President Bashar al-Asad. This occasion is marked by the preparations for the National Conference of the Bath Party, that will be preceded or followed by the formation of a new government, as well as the end of the Tenth Five Year Plan, and the preparation and adoption of the Eleventh Five-Year Plan.

During the past ten years, Syria has faced many difficult conditions on the foreign policy front which it managed with great success thanks to the leadership of Mr. President.

While some belligerent forces bet on the failure of the Syrian leadership to deal with these challenges, facts have proven that Syria has been successful and effective in overcoming such difficulties. The attempts to isolate Syria have failed and Syria has proven again to be an indispensable actor in any attempt to find solutions to the problems of the region.

But unlike the successes in foreign policy, to which Mr President has given his utmost interest due to its urgency and sensitivity, the management of the domestic situation at the political and economic levels, which are the responsibility of the executive administration as well as of other state institutions, has not achieved the same level of success. This has led to achievements on the external front and weakened the capacity of the state on the domestic front.

Domestic policy faced a number of difficulties that have escalated, by neglect and mismanagement, into a socio-economic crisis. This has resulted in a great deal of dissatisfaction among the citizens as well as the elite.

1 - Executive Summary:

- The first ten years of leadership of the President were marked by a broad shift in Syria's economic and political environment, and, to some extent, in the overall direction of its internal policy.
- Mr President set out, for the first time, the outlines of this change in his speech in July 2000 which has been reaffirmed in subsequent speeches, especially in the second inaugural speech in July 2007.

At the level of the structure of governance of the state:

- The structure of the Syrian state was formed in the 1960s and the 1970s, influenced by the Soviet model.
- This structure also fulfilled a historic role, but started to become obsolete causing an increased weakening in the role of these institutions (i.e. the party, the [National Progressive] Front, legislative power, the judiciary, the executive, mass organizations, business organizations and the role of different social factions and classes).
- Currently there are real questions about the centre of decision-making in Syria.
- At the level of state institutions, a major degradation of their role has been due to their failure in coping with drastic changes, rendering impossible, sometimes, the fulfilment of their function.
- Similarly at the level of administrative performance, which has witnessed a drastic deterioration of its functions, there has been a sclerosis or decrease in productivity, characterised by poor efficiency, low performance, and corruption.
- Perhaps the root of many of Syria's internal problems lies in the weakness and the sharp fall in administrative performance at the level of the executive (owing to bureaucracy, a lack of

accountability and corruption) as well as at the level of municipal and local state institutions.
- The main problem resides in the fact that these institutions are the very tools which are supposed to lead development and modernization.
- This has led in its turn to a fundamental weakness in the mobilizing capacity of the socio-political system. It has led as well to the paralysis of the state in its capability of managing the domestic file.
- Consequently there is an urgent need to redefine the roles and structure of these institutions, either at the vertical or horizontal level.

On the economic front:

- Syria began the transition from a socialist planned totalitarian economy with all its known characteristics some time ago.
- While a socialist economy fulfilled a historical role, it was no longer able to promote economic and social development.
- In addition, change was needed to cope with the international pressure Syria was facing in the context of a radical neo-liberal wave of globalization.
- Syria has shifted towards a market economy taking into account the political, economic, historic and cultural transformation that this entails.
- The Syrian route to a social market economy, however, has not simply conformed to an imported prefabricated prescription. It was perceived that reform could take many forms and tracks which have subsequently led to very different economic and social results.
- It is important to note that the Syrian institutions did not have any prior experience in dealing with or tackling a market economy.
- Moreover, Syria has embarked on the process of self-transformation without any assistance or support, but has been subjected, instead, to increasing external pressures. This has added new difficulties to the intrinsic problems of

- the transition itself, and has had negative implications in the shaping of economic, social and political developments.
- Therefore executive steps for policy reform, development and transition to a market-based economy in the recent past have taken a very selective approach.
- These steps were intentionally slowed down to avoid the risk of acceleration and destabilization in an atmosphere of a lack of experience and the exposure to external pressures.
- However, while this approach has resulted in some positive results, it has also had some negative consequences or effects that will impact on the shaping of future economic and social developments.
- This approach has not been balanced in terms of productivity, as it has focused on the liberalization of rent and financial sectors (finance and trade) and neglected productive sectors generating added value and employment opportunities (agriculture, industry, transport, tourism, construction, etc.).
- Subsequently, there have been some signs of social imbalance, where the support and protection provided by the state to the less fortunate classes has been reduced, while it has not been able to compensate for the regression of the role of the state as a welfare safety network.
- On the other hand, the Syrian private sector has demonstrated a lack of social responsibility and, at the same time, suffers from structural deficits that render it incapable of replacing the role of the state vis-à-vis the workers. Subsequently the private sector has been unable to fill the vacuum created by the retreat of the state
- The failure of the media sector in reaching the grass roots of the society and appealing to common sense in promoting the program of the president among the people has meant that most people only are seeing the regression of social support and the raising of prices. It seems to many that the state is abandoning the poor for the sake of the rich.
- The negative economic effects have started to show. The volume of imports has surpassed exports, and the trade deficit has begun to grow which has had a heavy impact on industry and other sectors.
- Furthermore, the negative results of this policy are apparent in the decrease in living standards and increased poverty rates. Figures in 2009 were higher than in 2004.

- Parallel to this, a drastic collapse in health services, education and transport has continued, in addition to growing corruption and bureaucracy, which have made people's quality of life unbearable.
- Some officials have said "that this is the price of reform, and this price must be paid." This justification has its risks, especially in a country like Syria which is exposed to various pressures, because the people may answer: "Those who are making money should pay the costs [of economic reforms]" and those who are making money are seen to be the government's clients. It is of utmost necessity to reconsider the recent economic policy and its outcomes in order to create a balanced productive economy and society.
- Recent economic steps have been characterized by a specific neo-liberal market economy, while what is required is to apply "a Syrian edition of the social market economy", which forms the core vision of the presidency.

Society:

- Society is becoming characterised by the emergence of an increasing social polarization.
- Cultural polarization is also becoming evident.
- There has been a decline in the principles of nationalism, secularism and liberal ideology.
- This has been coupled with a decline in the role of the state in social and communal management.
- This has subsequently provided an open field for salafist forces.
- Institutions based on pre-citizenship solidarities and primordial loyalties such as clans, tribes, ethnic and confessional groups have become more entrenched, and at the expense of national citizenship affiliation.

In conclusion:

- We have a young President but outmoded tools for development and modernization.
- We need new locomotives towing economic and social development

- Now, a decade after the arrival of the President to power, sufficient experience has been gained which is necessary to reconsider the path to modernisation.
- In order to develop this approach and move forward to the next period and prepare for the coming years ahead of Mr President, it is important to draw from the experiences of the past decade and to highlight the need for an overview of what has been achieved and what has not yet been achieved.

An aging state build-up and aging modes of management:

Four decades have passed since the corrective movement in which the basis and institutions of the modern Syrian state were established. This structure and the role of the entailing institutions have been affected to a large extent by the experience of relations with the former Soviet Union, politically, economically and socially.

Despite the significant developments that have taken place internally, regionally and internationally, the structure of the state has remained the same, where different state actors continue to play the same role. Any reform requires structural changes in the institutions and roles.

Ideas, ideologies, organizations and ways of thinking are born, grow strong, then gradually get old and require renewal.

This fact has created an imbalance on two levels: **The first level:** The overall structure of state institutions and the rules. And at **the second level:** of administrative performance of those various institutions.

The first level: due to great developments, the role of many institutions has changed in practice by virtue of natural development or due to a change in function and changes on the socio-economic structures.

The effectiveness of the Baath Party has been extensively weakened and it has practically lost its leadership role both in terms of rallying the people around the policies of the party or through auditing the state institutions. The Front parties have only had a negligible role, while the weakness of political life and activity in the community is the reason behind the reluctance of most people to participate in the process of modernization and development.

Subsequently, the role of national, secular and liberal forces has regressed. On the other hand, the domestic arena has been left to Salafist forces preaching their ideology in the guise of religion. Their power and influence have increased within the community and is still growing strongly.

Meanwhile the municipal and local authorities have further been weakened at the level of grassroots and their role has not been renewed or substituted for. Political and social competition for the leadership in those institutions has become completely absent. Absent as well are electoral programs and electoral auditing. This in turn has rendered institutions such as parliament and municipalities, local councils, trade unions, peasant organizations, women's groups, youth or student societies and the state media so weak that they have become a burden on the state instead of helping in the communication between the society and the state. Consequently, the capacity of these social instruments to curb and mend social and economic contradictions and conflict has been eroded.

The same goes for the performance of the executive branches of the bureaucracy. In turn, this has led to a lack of confidence of the citizens and to the decline in the role of these institutions as a major component of the safety network in the community. Such a decline has also impacted on the security services and their ability to deal with the society with tools other than violence.

Because of these aging institutions and the lack of clarity in their role, many questions have been raised within Syria and abroad about where the decision making and management of domestic issues takes place. Is it at the level of the regional command, the government or the office of the President?

Many thinkers and researchers agree on the importance of this question. While many officials point their fingers at the President asking him to take responsibility, the President himself has always insisted on the need to empower the state and its institutions.

The need for these institutions (the party, youth organisations, the National Progressive Front, government institutions, trade unions and other mass organizations, the media, education institutions, etc.) is more important today and in the future than it used to be in the past. They are the management tools at the domestic level. The efficiency and effectiveness of these (soft power) tools is of a vital importance, not only in raising the efficiency of the community, developing the Syrian state, and in helping to shape the Syrian reform, but also in helping the implementation of political, economic, social and cultural rights, and to strengthen the domestic resolve.

It should be noted that the potential use of hard power (police, security and military) in managing social problems is limited and risks inciting an international intervention in the internal affairs of the Syria state.

Hence, this requires a reconsideration of the roles of these organizations that constitute the basis of the state to suit the requirements of the future and the new vision for the country that would make Syria a model in all fields at both the Arab and regional levels.

The second level: relates to performance of the administrative body which suffers from regression, low efficiency, poor performance, low productivity and corruption. Perhaps the root of many of Syria's internal problems lies in the weakness of the capacities of the government, ministries and different state institutions to manage the domestic issues and to address the economic and social challenges.

The ministries have kept their old habits, without daring to take any decisions, preferring to evade responsibility, waiting, as they say, for instructions from above.

A further weakness resides in the lack of clarity and poor decision-making mechanisms, as well as in the weak management, implementation and follow-up of the ministries. These institutions support the old ineffective system of wages and recompenses, repelling every talent, failing to reward production and achievements, and lack objective criteria for the promotion of medium and higher elites. They also lack punishment and reward policies, and have widened the circle of corruption in the absence of any auditing system.

In sum, these defects clearly highlight many aspects of the weaknesses of different state institutions, without exception.

Experience has shown in the past decade that these institutions, that should have been the main tools of reform and modernization, have not been able to develop ideas and implement them into practice, whether they are institutions from the National Front or the parties, government bodies, state institutions, trade unions and other mass organizations they have all lost their effectiveness. This has negatively affected all of society.

Thus, the previous momentum inherited from the 1960s and 1970s, has slowed down due to objective factors, and must be replaced with new forces produced by new engines of change to generate the speed and power required for the new phase to come. This will only be achieved by redrawing the roles of these institutions as engines for reform to make them strong enough to realize the vision of reform and development for the shaping of a modern, strong and prosperous Syria.

2 - An imbalance in the economic approach:

There is no doubt that the steps of economic reform towards a market economy have achieved some positive results which would not have been possible without this reform. This was based on encouraging the private sector and incorporating the tens of thousands of Syrians entrepreneurs into productive economic activity. It has, also, attracted capital to Syria.

Much of this capital was Syrian capital that had been transferred abroad but it also included Arab and foreign investments that have created productive capacities and employment opportunities, improved the business climate, improved the legislative, regulatory structure, and improved Syrian experience in dealing with the international market.

Some private industries have been established and some have shown exports capacity. They have led to the improvement of tourism and of Syrian international economic relations, especially within the Arab arena as well as with Turkey.

It has been possible therefore to keep a relatively strong Syrian currency, and the budget deficit under control and external indebtedness low. It would not have been possible to achieve what has been achieved if Syria had continued its previous approach.

However, the market economy – without submitting Syria to a single prefabricated model – can take many forms with quite different economic and social results.

On one hand, Syrian institutions do not have the necessary experience in the market economy, on the other, the political conditions imposed on Syria meant that Syria has had to pursue its self-transformation without assistance and without any support.

Instead of receiving help and support Syria has faced external threats and challenges. This has added new difficulties to the transition itself, which have implications on the social and political spheres.

Although the government's plans for reforms were outlined for the first time in the Presidential speech in July 2000 and reaffirmed in later speeches, especially in the second inaugural speech in July 2007, the policy of reform and development and the transition to a market-based economy afterward has taken an experimental approach. For many reasons, an integrated, clearly defined strategy has not been pursued. Such an integrated approach is however necessary as directives for the reform of various institutions indicated in the state plan. The slow pace of reform was meant to avoid the risk of accelerating an uncontrolled reform process under conditions of a lack of experience and exposure to pressure. However, this experimental approach, which could have been justified, has resulted in some negative impact. It seems to us, that there is a need to reform the processes of economic decision making.

The new economic approach, for more than one reason, has not fulfilled its promises on many levels, and it has been unable to maintain and defend the benefits of the social safety network for the public. This is an important factor in preserving a sense of social satisfaction and loyalty for a wide range of the population. Instead, it has created dissatisfaction in many fields.

The reason for this difficulty is due to the lack of definite orientation towards a social market economy. The currently chosen track for reform simply ignores the needs of the less fortunate classes in our society, in spite of the fact that there are many other kinds of reform and many alternatives which could differ in their socio-economic outcome.

We think that the Tenth Five Year Plan has failed to achieve its objectives at an acceptable level. It has failed to control the high rate of population growth, failed to promote the job creation, and failed to tackle unemployment, despite some improvement. Subsequently Syria has not benefited from the oil boom in the region, which lasted from 2004 to 2008, and has not attracted sufficient investment.

Prices are soaring and have not been coupled with an increase in wages since 2006. Furthermore we must highlight the deficit in the trade balance in the global budget which is doomed to further increase with the decline in oil production.

The trade balance deficit for commodities for the year 2009 amounted to about 130 billion Syrian pounds (720 billion exports against 850 billion in imports), while the value of the state reserve of hard currency has declined, and agricultural production, which is still at the mercy of rains due to the failure in the plans for the transition to a modern irrigation system is also in decline. On the other side, industry in its turn is experiencing the pressures of the liberalization of imports.

On top of all these difficulties is the global financial crisis which has created additional pressure on the economic performance, investment, exports and unemployment.

Furthermore, the decline in social services, the shortage in electricity, the increasing numbers of people with no access to potable water, and the continued transport crisis all over the country have exacerbated popular disaffection. This has been compounded by the decline in health services and public hospitals infected by sluggishness and corruption, the extremely overcrowded public universities and the rise in organized crime and corruption, which remains widespread without any level of auditing.

A significant example of this is in the processing of the diesel fuel problem, a clear case that shows the inefficiency of the state administration in dealing with domestic issues. This is damaging the reputation of the state among the citizens.

The current edition of the market-based economy seems to be unbalanced and, far from favouring production, does not enhance the productivity capacity of the economy. The cabinet has tried to promote a market economy through liberalizing the finance and trade sectors. These sectors live on the productive sectors rather than being themselves productive in comparison with other areas of the economy producing real added value and income as well as jobs (such as industry, agriculture, transportation, construction amongst others). Competitiveness and liberalization have not been implemented in these productive sectors. In fact, the programs for the reform of the productive sectors have not been translated into reality at any level. This is reflected in our assessment of the Tenth Five-Year Plan.

Further, the pace of trade liberalization has been harmful to the productive sectors, such as industry. This seems to be an approach based on the recommendations of the International Monetary Fund, which is a recipe with known results at the social and economic level. In contrast, experiences in Japan and the Asian Tigers, and more recently in China, India and Brazil have shown they focused on the development of their productive sectors (especially industry) and the formulation of fiscal and monetary policies and trade to benefit the growth of these sectors. However in Syria economic policy has favoured traders at the expense of industrialists, leading many of the latter to shift from productive activities to commercial activities and rent. This has been at the expense of the productive capacity of the Syrian economy.

The private sector in Syria has for the most part not flourished and matured yet. It does not recognize its ethical, social and national responsibilities either in terms of implementing the new modes of production or fulfilling its social obligations. The private sector does not comply with its moral and social responsibilities which guide the business sectors in developed countries. Its commitment to the rule of law is very weak, it continues to evade taxes and to avoid payment of customs duties and social security duties through bribes. It does not care about the environment or for workers' rights, and pays no attention to improving the working conditions or the conditions of residence of workers and their families. Nor does it understand the importance of the company as a social institution, rather than being the property of an individual acting out his desires. The private sector does not contribute to the projects of private welfare, such as the granting of scholarships for students, the establishment of health centres and the support of sports, as well as cultural and artistic activities. It does not care for people with special needs or of scientific research. It should share responsibility for all with the state.

On the other hand, the state treasury has lost a lot of its capacity and resources, due to lower rents and the decline in both the oil surplus and foreign aid. Unless the government works hard to offset this with taxes, there could be no solution to the problem of the lack of revenue. The problem of low tax revenue from the private sector is crucial as the majority of Treasury revenues from taxes come from the oil or the public sector. Tax evasion is still widespread, despite the significant reductions made in tax rates, to the extent that they have become less than the rate of taxes in major capitalist countries. The government has not made any efforts to combat smuggling and customs evasion, which drains the state treasury of large sums.

The government has not taken the initiative in over ten years to reform the public sector so as to get rid of losses in public enterprises either in the so-called non-strategic or strategic installations. Nothing has been done to repair and rehabilitate its facilities and to restore competitiveness, or to allow financial and administrative independence and flexibility in public firms. This decline has led to a further reduction the income from the public sector. This situation has weakened the ability of the public treasury and therefore the state, to continue playing its role, to bear the same burdens. It has led to a decline in its ability to implement reform.

In other countries where a market economy has been applied, great importance is given to the balance in society, in order to maintain social stability (between the power of state institutions, business organizations and workers in trade unions). In Syria, an increasing concentration of power in the hands of the crony bureaucracy classes is notable, while the popular classes have lost power. Such a phenomenon has its risks, especially in a country like Syria, which is exposed to various external pressures. The need to ensure the loyalty of the population is of utmost importance.

The social contract allowing the Baath party to apply the principle of a balance of classes, and to neutralize the resistance of feudalism and capital was based on the alliance between the workers, peasants, small income earners and educated revolutionaries, as well as the promotion and development of the public sector. Also important was the ownership of small and medium enterprises, the redistribution of territory of large landowners to farmers, taking into account the interests of the producing classes, the most vulnerable in the community, and the expansion of free education in the depths of the countryside and the poor neighbourhoods.

This led to the creation of social mobility and broadly enabled large groups of the vulnerable in rural and urban areas to climb the social ladder and to access vital positions in the state and society (among them educated groups, senior government officials, university professors, engineers, doctors, officers, leaders, and others).

This created a strong loyalty to the Baath regime between these broad categories in addition to the peasantry and workers. This was reflected during the confrontations with the Muslim Brotherhood as well as in the mass mobilization for the October Liberation War, the intervention in Lebanon to end the civil war and the failure of the Israeli invasion.

The decomposition of the social safety network is however evident in the abolition of the protection of rented houses, the abolition of the protection of peasant land, the elimination of worker rights, the reduction of subsidized prices, the freezing of wages and the halt on the expansion of the public sector which have all prevented the reform from creating alternative institutions to compensate for the damage caused to the most vulnerable sectors in society.

The private sector has not succeeded in creating tangible benefits or provided solutions to these problems. It has not been able to create enough jobs to absorb new entrants into the labour market or protect workers. It has been unable to develop large industrial sectors or to pay higher wages. It is not interested in its social duties. This has given the impression to the poorer classes that the state "is giving up its historical alliances and is biased in favour of the rich at the expense of the poor".

These poorer social classes have been and will remain a key bloc of citizens whose support is important in this transformation. The current policy is narrowing the base of the regime and makes the system unable to activate these classes when they are needed in the internal and external confrontations.

If we add this to the decline in state capacity and the lack of willingness to support free education, medical care and subsidies, this will lead to further polarization of the community, something which threatens social stability. This will also lead to the erosion of the middle class and reverse its role as a dynamo in the society.

If we add this polarization to the cultural polarization, the risks appear doubled. The Syrian community is witnessing the growth of cultural division, including those among youth groups. In light of the significant decline of the identity and ideology of the state, and the Baath Party as a secular nationalist party, more and more splits will occur. The community will be torn apart between the Salafist groups and the forces of modernization. This division is further amplified by the new cyberspace. With the growing sentiments of tribalism and sectarianism the new generation is fragmented and desperate.

Conclusions

The past ten years have witnessed successes in the management of foreign policy but have not been matched by similar success in the management of internal policy. This is due to the weakness in the development of state tools, the erosion in the role of traditional institutions and the weakness in the capacity of government and state institutions.

The situation can be summarized as: an ambitious young President, a rising young generation with immense needs, difficult domestic and international conditions, and a continuing failure of the tools of state for the efficient implementation of reform. This requires a comprehensive vision for the present and for the future to create an effective mechanism to cope with the aspirations of the leadership. The time is right, as foreign policy success gives the opportunity to focus on the internal situation.

---

[1] Translation from Arabic by a member of the advisory committee. The authors have been assured anonymity.

References

Abu-Lughod, Lila (2005) *Dramas of Nationhood: The Politics of Television in Egypt* (Chicago: University of Chicago Press).
Alberoni, Francesco (1972) "The Powerless 'Elite': Theory and Sociological Research on the Phenomenon of the Stars", in Redmond, Sean and Homes, Su (2007, eds.) *Stardom and Celebrity: A Reader* (London: Sage).
Alonso, Andoni & Oiarzaba, Pedro G. (2010, eds.) *Diasporas in a New Media Age: Identity, Politics, and Community* (Nevada: University of Nevada Press).
Amnesty International Report (2011) "The Long Reach Of The Mukhabaraat: Violence And Harassment Against Syrians Abroad And Their Relatives Back Home" (London: Amnesty International Publications).
Anderson, Benedict (2006) *Imagined Communities: Reflections on the Origin and Spread of Nationalism* (London: Verso).
Anderson, Jon W. (1997) "Cybernauts of the Arab Diaspora: Electronic Mediation in Transnational Cultural Identities", prepared for Couch-Stone Symposium, Postmodern Culture, Global Capitalism and Democratic Action, University of Maryland (10-12 April 1997).
- (2008) "Mediatized Islam, Cyberspace and the Public Sphere", Prepared for Conference on "The Challenges of Integrating Islam: Comparative Experiences of Europe and the Middle East", Institute for Middle East Studies, George Washington University (February 14, 2008).
Appadurai, Arjun (1996) *Modernity at Large: Cultural Dimensions of Globalization* (Minneapolis: University of Minnesota Press).
Armburst, Walter (2007) "New Media and Old Agendas: The Internet in the Middle East and Middle Eastern Studies", *International Journal of Middle East Studies*, Vol. 39, Issue 4.pp. 531-533.
Ayish, Muhammad Ibrahim (2008) *The new Arab public sphere* (Berlin: Frank and Timme).
Basch, Linda; Schiller, Nina Glick; & Szanton-Blanc, Crista (1994) *Nations Unbound: Transnational Projects, Postcolonial Predicaments and Deterritorialized Nation-States* (London and New York: Routledge).
Brah, Avtar (1996) *Cartographies of Diaspora: Contesting Identities* (London and New York: Routledge)
Calhoun, Craig (1990) (eds.) *Habermas and the Public Sphere* (Cambridge, MA and London: MIT Press).
- (1995) *Critical Social Theory: Culture, History, and the Challenge of Difference* (Oxford: Blackwell).

Castells, Manuel (2008) "The New Public Sphere: Global Civil Society, Communication Networks, and Global Governance" *The ANNALS of the American Academy of Political and Social Science*, Vol. 616, No. 1. pp. 78-93.

Chalala, Elie (2011) "Light vs. Darkness: How the Syrian Opposition & Assad Regime Approach the Media", *Al-Jadid*, Vol. 16, no. 62.

Cooke, Miriam (2007) *Dissident Syria: Making Oppositional Arts Official* (Durham and London: Duke University Press).

Cottle, Simon (2011) "Media and the Arab uprisings of 2011: Research notes", *Journalism,* Vol. 11. No. 5. pp. 647-659.

De Certau, Michel (1984) *The Practice of Everyday Life* (London: The University of California Press).

Dubowitz, Mark et al. (2011) *U.S. Policy in Syria: Testimony for Senate Foreign Relations Committee*. Foundation for Defense of Democracies. 9 November. Available at: http://www.defenddemocracy.org/testimony/us-policy-in-syria#sthash.gD33H9eg.dpuf.

Dyer, Richard and McDonald, Paul (1998) *Stars* (London: British Film Institute).

Eickelman, Dale & Salvatore, Armando (2006) (eds.), *Public Islam and the Common Good* (Leiden: Brill).

Eickelman, Dale and Anderson, Jon (2003) *New Media in the Muslim World: The Emerging Public Sphere* (Bloomington: Indiana University Press).

Fraser, Nancy (1991) "Rethinking the Public Sphere: A Contribution to the Critique of Actually Existing Democracy" in Calhoun, Craig (ed.) *Habermas and the Public Sphere* (Cambridge, MA: MIT Press).

- (2007) "Transnationalizing the Public Sphere: On the Legitimacy and Efficacy of Public Opinion in a Post-Westphalian World", *Theory Culture Society* Vol. 24 No. 7. pp. 7-30.

George, Alan (2003) *Syria: Neither Bread nor Freedom* (London: Zed Books).

Ghadbian, Najib (forthcoming) "Contesting Authoritarianism: Opposition Activism under Bashar Asad" In: Raymond Hinnebusch & Tina Zintl (eds.) *Syria under Bashar al-Asad, 2000-2010: Political Economy and International Relations* (New York: Syracuse University Press).

Graham, Mark & Khosravi, Shahram (2002) "Reordering Public and Private in Iranian Cyberspace: Identity, Politics and Mobilization", *Identities: Global Studies in Culture and Power*, Vol. 9, No. 2. pp. 219-246.

Guidry, John A.; Kennedy, Michael D.; & Zald, Mayer N. (2001) (eds.) *Globalizations and Social Movements: Culture, Power, and the Transnational Public Sphere* (Ann Arbor: University of Michigan Press).

Habermas, Jürgen (1989) *The Structural Transformation of the Public Sphere* (Cambridge, MA and London: MIT Press).

Hinnebusch, Raymond (2004) "Syria after the Iraq War: Between the Neo-con Offensive and Internal Reform," *DOI-Focus* No. 14.

Hirst, David (2010) *Beware of Small States* (London: Faber and Faber).

Holmes, Su (2005) "'Starring ... Dyer?': Re-visiting Star Studies and Contemporary Celebrity Culture", *Westminster Papers in Communication and Culture*, Vol. 2, Issue 2, pp. 6-21.

International Crises Group (2011) "Popular Protests in North Africa and the Middle East (VII): The Syrian Regime's Slow-motion Suicide", Middle East Report No. 109, (13 July, 2011) Amman/Brussels.

International Crisis Group (2004), "Syria under Bashar (II): Domestic Policy Challenges", Middle East Report No. 23/24, (11 February, 2004) Amman/Brussels.

Ismail, Salwa (2011) "Silencing the Voice of Freedom in Syria", *Index on Censorship*, 8 July 2011, available on www.indexoncensorship.org/2011/07/silencing-the-voice-of-freedom-in-syria.

Karim, Karim H. (2003) *The Media of Diaspora* (London and New York: Routledge).

Khamis, Sahar & Vaughn, Katherine (2011) "Cyberactivism in the Egyptian Revolution: How Civic Engagement and Citizen Journalism Tilted the Balance", *Arab Media and Society*, Issue 13.

Kraidy, Marwan M. (2010) *Reality Television and Arab Politics: Contention in Public Life* (Cambridge: Cambridge University Press).

- (2006) "Syria: Media Reform and Its Limitations, *Arab Reform Bulletin*, Vol.4, Issue. 4 (May), no page numbers.

Kuebler, Johanne (2011) "Overcoming the Digital Divide: The Internet and Political Mobilization in Egypt and Tunisia" *CyberOrient*, Vol. 5, Issue. 1.

Landis, Joshua & Pace, Joe (2009) "The Syrian Opposition: The Struggle for Unity and Relevance, 2003-2008" in Lawson, Fred H. (ed.) *Demystifying Syria* (London: SAQI and Middle East Institute SOAS).

- (2006) "The Syrian Opposition", *The Washington Quarterly*, Vol. 30, No.1, pp. 45-68.

Landzelius, Kyra (1999) (ed.), *Native on the Net: Indigenous Cyber-activism and Virtual Diasporas over the World Wide* Web (London: Routledge).

Lawson, Fred H. (2010) *Demystifying Syria* (London: Saqi Books).

Leverett, Flynt (2005) *Inheriting Syria: Bashar's Trial by Fire* (Washington, D.C.: Brookings Institution Press).

Lynch, Mark (2006) *Voices of the New Arab Public* (New York: Columbia University Press).

Mahmood, Saba (2005) *The Politics of Piety: The Islamic Revival and the Feminist Subject* (Princeton: Princeton University Press).

Mandaville, Pete (2001)*Transnational Muslim Politics: Reimagining the Umma* (London: Routledge).

Ma'oz, Moshe (1988) *Asad: The Sphinx of Damascus: A Political Biography* (London Weidenfeld & Nicolson).

Mitchell, Katharyne (1997) "Different Diasporas and the Hype of Hybridity", *Environment and Planning D: Society and Space* Vol. 15, Issue. 5. pp. 533-553.

Nagel, Caroline & Staeheli, Lynn (2010) "ICT and geographies of British Arab and Arab American activism", *Global Networks* Vol. 10, Issue 2, pp. 262–281.

Noman, Helmi (2011) "The Emergence of Open and Organized Pro-Government Cyber Attacks in the Middle East: The Case of the Syrian Electronic Army", *Information Warfare Monitor* (May 30, 2011).

Olesen, Thomas (2005) "Transnational Publics: New Spaces of Social Movement Activism and the Problem of Global Long-Sightedness, *Current Sociology*, Vol. 53. No. 3. pp. 419-440

Ong, Aihwa (2003) "Cyberpublics and Diaspora Politics Among Transnational Chinese", *Interventions*, Vol. 5, Issue. 1, pp. 82-100.

Perthes, Volker (1995) *The Political Economy of Syria under Asad* (London: I.B. Tauris).

Rinnawi, Khalil (2010) "'Cybernaut' Diaspora: Arab Diaspora in Germany", in Andoni Alonso & Pedro G. Oiarzaba (eds.) *Diasporas in a New Media Age: Identity, Politics, and Community* (Nevada: University of Nevada Press), pp. 265-290.

Robertson, Roland (1995) "Glocalization: Time-Space and Homogeneity-Heterogeneity", in Featherstone, Mike; Lash, Scott; & Robertson, Roland (eds.) *Global Modernities* (London: Sage) pp. 25-44.

Rojek, Chris (2001) *Celebrity* (London: Reaktion Books).

Sabry, Tarik (2011, ed.) *Arab Cultural Studies, Mapping the Field* (London: I.B. Tauris).

Salamandra, Christa (2000) "Consuming Damascus: Public Culture and the Construction of Social Identity", in Walter Armbrust (ed.) *Mass Mediations: New Approaches to Popular Culture in the Middle East and Beyond* (London: University of California Press).

Salamandra, Christa (2004) *A New Old Damascus: Authenticity and Distinction in Urban Syria* (Bloomington: Indiana University Press).

Sassen, Saskia (1999) "Digital networks and power", in Featherstone, Mike & Lash, Scott (eds.) *Spaces of Culture: City, Nation, World* (London: Sage). pp. 49–63.

Seale, Patrick (1988) *The Struggle for the Middle East* (London: I.B. Tauris).

Seifan, Samir (2010) *Syria on the Path of Economic Reform*, St. Andrew's Papers on Contemporary Syria (St Andrews/Fife and Boulder: Lynne Rienner Publishers).

Shaery-Eisenlohr, Roschanack (2011) "From Subjects to Citizens? Civil Society and the Internet in Syria", *Middle East Critique*, Vol. 20, Issue 2. pp. 127-138.

Staeheli, Lynn A.; Ledwith, Valerie; Ormond, Meghann; Reed, Katie; Sumpter, Amy; & Trudeau, Daniel (2002) "Immigration, the internet, and spaces of politics", *Political Geography* 21: pp. 989–1012.

Tölölyan, Kachig (1996) "Rethinking Diaspora(s): Stateless Power in the Transnational Moment", *Diaspora: A Journal of Transnational Studies*, Vol. 5, No. 1, pp. 3-36.

Tripp, Charles (2001) "State, Elites and the 'Management of Change" in Hakimian, Hasan & Moshaver, Ziba (eds.) *The State and Global Change: The Political Economy of Transition in the Middle East and North Africa* (London: Curzon) pp. 211–231

Turner, Graeme (2010) Approaching Celebrity Studies, *Celebrity Studies*, Vol. 1, issue 1, pp. 11-20.

Van Dam, Nikolaos (2011^4) *The Struggle for Power in Syria* (London: IB Tauris).

Van De Donk, Wim; Loader, Brian & Rucht, Dieter (2003) (eds.) *Cyberprotest: New Media, Citizens and Social Movements* (London: Routledge).

Van Den Bos, Matthijs & Nell, Liza (2006) "Territorial bounds to virtual space: transnational online and offline networks of Iranian and Turkish-Kurdish immigrants in the Netherlands", *Global Networks*, Vol. 6, Issue 2. pp.201-220

Vertovec, Steven (1999) "Conceiving and researching transnationalism", *Ethnic and Racial Studies*, Vol. 22, Issue 2. pp. 447-462.
- (2003) "Diaspora, Transnationalism and Islam: Sites of Change and Modes of Research" in Stefano Allievi & Jørgen Nielsen (eds.) *Muslim Networks and Transnational Communities in and across Europe* (Leiden, Boston: Brill).
Wedeen, Lisa (1999) *Ambiguities of Domination: Politics, Rhetoric, and Symbols in Contemporary Syria* (Chicago: University of Chicago Press).
- (2008) *Peripheral Visions: Publics, Power, and Performance in Yemen* (Chicago: University of Chicago Press).
Weyman, George (2006) "Empowering Youth or Reshaping Compliance? Star Magazine, Symbolic Production, and Competing Visions of Shabab in Syria", M.Phil Thesis in Modern Middle Eastern Studies, Wadham College, University of Oxford.
Wieland, Carsten (2006) *Syria - Ballots or Bullets? Democracy, Islamism, and Secularism in the Levant* (Seattle: Cune Press).

Newspapers and websites

Al-Akhbar Newspaper (http://www.al-akhbar.com)
Al-Arabiyya (www.alarabiya.net)
Bloomberg (www.bloomberg.com)
Al-Jazeera; al-Jazeera English www.aljazeera.com/
The Daily Star (www.dailystar.com.lb)
Discover Syria (www.discover-syria.com)
The Economist
www.facebook.com
Foreign Policy www.foreignpolicy.com
Forward Magazine
www.france24.com/
Frankfurter Allgemeine Zeitung
The Guardian (www.guardian.co.uk)
Al-Hayat
www.independent.co.uk
www.internetworldstats.com
www.joshualandis.com
Mideast Views (www.mideastviews.com)
www.msnbc.msn.com
Naharnet Newsdesk (www.naharnet.com)
The New York Times Magazine (http://www.nytimes.com)
www.newyorker.com/
www.nowlebanon.com
www.online.wsj.com
Reuters (www.reuters.com)
Rossiya 1 TV
www.rferl.org/
Al-Safir
Syrian Arab News Agency (www.sana.sy)
Al-Sharq Al-Awsat
www.shiachat.com/

Der Spiegel,
Süddeutsche Zeitung
Syria-News (http://www.syria-news.com)
Syrian Revolution Digest (http://www.syrianrevolutiondigest.com)
Syrian Times
Syria Today
www.SyriaTrash.com
www.twitter.com
http://trash.vsyria.com/
www.washingtonpost.com
www.worldcrunch.com/
Yedioth Internet (www.ynetnews.acom)

About the Authors

Adam Almqvist has a BA from the School of Oriental and African Studies, University of London and an MA in Middle Eastern Studies from Lund University, Sweden. During 2010-2012 he was a Research Assistant for the Syria Research Project at the Center for Middle Eastern Studies, Lund University and during 2012 he conducted research in Cairo among Syrian political refugees on a scholarship from the Swedish International Development Cooperation Agency.

Helena Nassif is a PhD candidate at the University of Westminster, London. Her research investigates the politics of mass culture in the Levant through the case study of Bab el-Hara, a hit Syrian television drama series. Helena is a former television journalist as well as a development professional and consultant. She recently published a chapter "Making Sense of War News among Adolescents in Lebanon" in Matar and Harb's edited collection *Narrating Conflict in the Middle East* (2013). Helena was a founding staff of the Arab Council for the Social Sciences in Beirut where she conceptualised and managed the research grants and fellowships awards programme. She is currently based in Cairo.

Carsten Wieland studied history, political science and philosophy at Humboldt University in Berlin (PhD in 1999), Duke University in North Carolina, and at Jawaharlal Nehru University in New Delhi. Since 2011, he works in the German Foreign Office. Before he entered the diplomatic career he worked as a political consultant, analyst, author and journalist and spent several years in the Middle East. Being a Syria expert for more than a decade, he published numerous articles and books on the Levant, amongst them *Syria at Bay: Secularism, Islamism, and "Pax Americana"*, Hurst, London in 2006. Carsten previously worked at the Goethe Institute in Cairo and Munich and as a country representative for the Konrad Adenauer Foundation in Colombia. He was a correspondent for the German Press Agency (DPA) in Washington, Tel

Aviv, and Colombia, as well as DPA head of corporate communications and public affairs in Berlin. He is guest professor for international relations at the Universidad del Rosario in Bogotá and was a fellow at the Public Policy Department at Georgetown University in Washington D.C. (www.carsten-wieland.de).